SOCIAL CAPITAL

The term 'social capital' is a way of conceptualising the intangible resources of community, shared values and trust upon which we draw in daily life. It has achieved considerable international currency in the social sciences through the very different work of Pierre Bourdieu in France and James Coleman and Robert Putnam in the United States and has been taken up within politics and sociology as a means of explaining the decline of social cohesion and community values in many western societies.

Social Capital is one of the first full overviews of the intense debate surrounding this subject. This clear and comprehensive introduction explains the theoretical underpinning of the subject, the empirical work that has been done to explore its operation, and the effect that it has had on policy making, particularly within such international governmental bodies as the World Bank and the European Commission.

John Field is Director of the Division of Academic Innovation and Continuing Education at the University of Stirling.

KEY IDEAS

SERIES EDITOR: PETER HAMILTON, THE OPEN UNIVERSITY, MILTON KEYNES

Designed to compliment the successful *Key Sociologists*, this series covers the main concepts, issues, debates and controversies in sociology and the social sciences. The series aims to provide authoritative essays on central topics of social science, such as community, power, work, sexuality, inequality, benefits and ideology, class, family, etc. Books adopt a strong individual 'line' constituting original essays rather than literary surveys, and for lively and original treatments of their subject matter. The books will be useful to students and teachers of sociology, political science, economics, psychology, philosophy and geography.

Citizenship
KEITH FAULKS

Class
STEPHEN EDGELL

Community
GERARD DELANTY

Consumption
ROBERT BOCOCK

Culture
CHRIS JENKS

Globalization – second edition
MALCOLM WATERS

Lifestyle
DAVID CHANEY

Mass Media
PIERRE SORLIN

Moral Panics
KENNETH THOMPSON

Old Age
JOHN VINCENT

Postmodernity
BARRY SMART

Racism – second edition
ROBERT MILES AND
MALCOLM BROWN

Risk
DEBORAH LUPTON

Sexuality
JEFFREY WEEKS

Social Capital
JOHN FIELD

Transgression
CHRIS JENKS

The Virtual
ROB SHIELDS

SOCIAL CAPITAL

John Field

Routledge
Taylor & Francis Group

LONDON AND NEW YORK

First published 2003
by Routledge
11 New Fetter Lane, London EC4P 4EE

Simultaneously published in the USA and Canada
by Routledge
29 West 35th Street, New York, NY 10001

Routledge is an imprint of the Taylor & Francis Group

© 2003 John Field

Typeset in Garamond and Scala by
Keystroke, Jacaranda Lodge, Wolverhampton
Printed and bound in Great Britain by
TJ International Ltd, Padstow, Cornwall

British Library Cataloguing in Publication Data
A catalogue record for this book is available from the British Library

Library of Congress Cataloging in Publication Data
A catalog record for this book has been requested

ISBN 0–415–25753–0 HB
ISBN 0–415–25754–9 PB

CONTENTS

Acknowledgements

Connections count, and many friends, colleagues and acquaintances have helped me develop my ideas about social capital. Much of this learning has been profoundly rewarding in itself. Trust and reciprocity are not just conceptual abstractions; they help make life rather more secure and pleasurable than it would otherwise have been. Equally, of course, at some stages in life I have found myself learning lessons about trust, reciprocity and loss that I could well have lived without. Many of us discover at some stage that while our closest and most valued ties often lend meaning and affirmation to our existence, they can also prove the cause of deep pain. Such everyday lessons – positive and negative – are writ large in our wider society. They have particularly informed the final chapter of this book, in which I reflect on what we might do as a society to promote forms of social capital that are appropriate for our own times.

Writing this book has benefited from countless exchanges with friends and colleagues, providing me with very particular examples of the ways that our connections are resources. Thoughtful conversations with Peter Alheit, Julie Allan, Colin Bell, Loraine Blaxter, Jaswinder Dhillon, Kathryn Ecclestone, Richard Edwards, Ian Falk, Tom Healy, Christina Hughes, Sue Kilpatrick, William Maloney, Michael Strain, Lorna Unwin and Bill Williamson made me look again at some of my weaker ideas. From Gudrun Geirsdottir I gleaned a fine Icelandic proverb. Pat Ainley and Tom Steele have tried to persuade me that social capital is a dead end or worse; they have failed (so far) but I have learned in the process. John Scott read an early draft and provided valuable feedback. Above all, I owe an enormous amount to three colleagues – Steve Baron, Tom Schuller and Simon Szreter – with whom I worked on the remarkably enjoyable seminar series on social capital sponsored by the Economic and Social Research Council, which ran during 2000 and 2001 in Cambridge, Glasgow, London and Warwick. These seminars built social capital as well as debating it, and I have lost track of the debts which I owe to the participants. Tom and Steve were also wonderful co-editors of a book of critical essays on social capital.

INTRODUCTION:
WHAT IS SOCIAL CAPITAL AND
WHY DOES IT MATTER?

The theory of social capital is, at heart, most straightforward. Its central thesis can be summed up in two words: relationships matter. By making connections with one another, and keeping them going over time, people are able to work together to achieve things that they either could not achieve by themselves, or could only achieve with great difficulty. People connect through a series of networks and they tend to share common values with other members of these networks; to the extent that these networks constitute a resource, they can be seen as forming a kind of capital. As well as being useful in its immediate context, this stock of capital can often be drawn on in other settings. In general, then, it follows that the more people you know, and the more you share a common outlook with them, the richer you are in social capital. This, in a nutshell, is the thesis that this book explores.

The concept of social capital is increasingly influential. It has taken off like a bushfire in the social sciences, it has started to catch on in policy circles, and it has also flared up from time to time in the mass media. While there is a spreading literature on the concept, though, there has so far been nothing in the way of an extended introduction. This book sets out to fill this gap. It gives an overview of the main ideas of the three outstanding theorists of social capital, and places these in the context of their authors' ideas about the world. It then sets out in more detail the ways in which social capital makes a difference to peoples' lives, positive and negative. It then asks whether social capital is changing, and if so, in what ways, as a result of the momentous transformations of our lives. It then tries to draw out the practical lessons of this analysis. It makes no attempt at providing a comprehensive discussion of the concept; this is a task which has yet to be tackled, and indeed is probably better conducted once we have a stronger evidence base on which to proceed. I have assumed that most readers will either have some basic grounding in social science or, if not, will be sufficiently interested to look up the basic ideas of thinkers such as Marx, Durkheim, Smith and Weber. Otherwise, the intention is to provide an accessible guide to an idea that has grasped the imagination of policy-makers and professionals in areas from business management to social policy, and influenced research and theory right across the social sciences.

HOW DO NETWORKS MAKE THINGS HAPPEN?

Modern organisations are governed by rules. There are accepted procedures for making or appealing decisions, and responsibilities are usually defined clearly in terms of a position rather than a person. But when they want to make something happen, many people will ignore these formal procedures and responsibilities, and set off to talk to someone they know. Important decisions almost always involve a degree of uncertainty and risk: if someone is looking for a new job or planning to appoint someone to a job, if they are looking for someone to service their car or mend the washing machine, if they are thinking of moving home or introducing a new way of organising the office, or if they want to find the best school or hospital, using the formal procedures is no guarantee of success. To make things happen, people often prefer to bypass the formal system and talk to people that they know. Calling on trusted friends, family or acquaintances is much less stressful than dealing with bureaucracies, and it usually seems to work faster and often produces a better outcome.

So people's networks really do count. As the cliché has it, it is not what you know that counts, but who you know. More accurately, it is of course both what and who you know that comes in handy. And just knowing people isn't enough if they don't feel obliged to help you. If people are going to help one another, they need to feel good about it, which means that they need to feel they have something in common with each other. If they do share values, they are much more likely to cooperate to achieve mutual goals. Formal systems – combining impersonal order and hierarchical rules – are often an attempt to control the excesses of mutual informal cooperation, which can lead to forms of indirect discrimination against others who do not belong in the charmed circle. Some networks, like the 'old boy networks' that are said to dominate parts of the British Civil Service and business leadership or the family-based *Chaebol* business networks of Korea, cooperate with the aim of keeping out those who do not wear the old school tie or come from the same kinship grouping. George Bernard Shaw, in a preface to his play *The Doctor's Dilemma*, famously said that all professions are a conspiracy against the public. Social relationships can sometimes serve to exclude and deny as well as include and enable.

People's networks should be seen, then, as part of the wider set of relationships and norms that allow people to pursue their goals, and also serve to bind society together. Anthony Giddens, the leading British sociologist, has based his theory of 'structuration' on the proposition that 'structure is always both enabling and constraining, in virtue of the inherent relation between structure and agency (and agency and power)' (Giddens 1984: 169). We can therefore expect that people may sometimes find that options are constrained by the nature of the resources that they can get hold of through their connections. At other times, they will use their networks to liberate them from other constraints. And at other times still, they will use their social capital to uphold their claims over those of others who are trying to access the same resources.

Membership of networks, and a set of shared values, are at the heart of the concept of social capital. Speaking about these social phenomena as a form of 'capital' is ambivalent. On the one hand, it points to their role as a resource, even as a source of power or influence, rooted deeply in specific social settings. Connections bring obligations to other people, but by the same token those people then acquire obligations to you. On the other hand, the concept is related to the human capital tradition of thinking about the economics of education, and the metaphor similarly points to ideas of investment, accumulation and exploitation that have been seized upon in such areas as global development and anti-poverty strategies or the study of business innovation and technological change.

Social capital has been widely discussed across the social sciences in recent years. Counting the number of academic articles appearing on a subject is perhaps not the most compelling way of understanding its wider appeal. For what it is worth, though, the number of journal articles listing social capital as a key word before 1981 totalled 20, and between 1991 and 1995 it rose to 109. Between 1996 and March 1999, the total was 1,003 (Harper 2001: 6), and the growth shows no sign of abating. On this index, then, we can safely speak of an explosion of scholarly interest in social capital. Yet, equally striking, a growing number of journalists and policy-makers are familiar with the term, which is starting to enter into the language of a wider public.

Robert D. Putnam, the American political scientist, can plausibly claim much of the credit for popularising what had previously been a rather obscure terminology, rescuing it from the abstraction of social and economic theory. In summary, Putnam has defined social capital as:

> features of social organisation, such as trust, norms, and networks, that can improve the efficiency of society by facilitating coordinated actions.
> (Putnam 1993a: 169)

This definition originally appeared in a study of political traditions in Italy, but Putnam's later work took the idea and applied it to the study of social connections in the United States (Putnam 2000). His central theme since the mid-1990s has been that, from the 1960s onwards, Americans have chosen steadily to withdraw from civic life. Putnam's ideas will be discussed in greater detail later on, as will those of others who have influenced the way the concept has developed or have tried to argue that it is not as useful as it might seem. But he is on his own in the way that his ideas have grabbed the attention of scholars, policy-makers and even the wider public. Love him or loathe him, Putnam has picked a topic – the collapse of social capital in America – that speaks to the hopes and fears of many people.

Putnam's gift for plain prose and vivid imagery has helped bring the idea to the attention of policy-makers and the wider public. A paper in a rather obscure specialist journal in 1995 bore the attention-catching title 'Bowling Alone', which Putnam then used once more for his lengthy book (Putnam 1995: 2001). The picture of bowling lanes peopled by individuals playing on their own – drawn from Putnam's evidence on the decline of league bowling in the USA – neatly captured the idea of people's steady disengagement from a common public life. Putnam also showed the zeal of a missionary, launching his book across two continents with a series of lively seminars for policy-makers, interviews in the broadsheet press, and appearances on the more serious radio and TV talk shows. Putnam is also a great simplifier, as the idea of the lonely bowler suggests. He believes that social capital is a Good Thing and that its collapse is a Bad Thing; he believes that there is one big villain (television) and many minor bad guys (cars, loss of free time, the aging of the generation that confronted the big collective challenges of war and depression); and he wants action to restore it to health. But as well as being a powerful communicator with passionate beliefs and a simple bottom line, Putnam is also a tireless social scientist who has marshalled a compelling body of evidence, and analysed it with care. He is sounding a tune that accords with the beliefs and experiences of many of his readers.

NORMS AND NETWORKS IN CLASSICAL SOCIAL THEORY

The quality of human relationships has long been a concern for social theorists. Putnam's preoccupations today are in many ways a mirror-image of those of many nineteenth-century social commentators. Reflecting on his travels throughout the United States in the 1831, the French writer Alexis de Tocqueville (1832) described in detail the vibrant associational life that underpinned American democracy and economic strength. For de Tocqueville, interaction in voluntary associations provided a social glue that helped to bond individual Americans together, in contrast to the formal bonds of status and obligation that held together the more traditional and hierarchical relationships that he was familiar with in Europe. Some sixty years after de Tocqueville's study appeared, a similar preoccupation with relationships as a source of meaning and order was echoed in the work of the pioneering French sociologist Emile Durkheim (1933), in his reflections on the long transition from what he described as the 'mechanical solidarity' of the feudal world to the 'organic solidarity' of nineteenth-century capitalism. For Durkheim, the former was mechanical because it was unthinking and habitual, based as it was on the fixed structures and obligations of lord and peasant, cleric and artisan. All knew their place, and they knew how others were placed as well. In capitalist, urban, industrial society, by contrast, people lived in a world of strangers, yet managed their affairs without the strictly regulated division of labour of feudalism. Rather, they entered into a multitude of connections that were based on a variety of interactions, each of which was entered into because it served a purpose. Similar concerns can be seen in Ferdinand Tönnies' attempt to distinguish between purposive association (which he termed *Gemeinschaft*, or community) and instrumental association (which he called *Gesellschaft*, or society). It might also to some extent be reflected in Max Weber's thought on authority and charisma, as well as in his emphasis on a shared 'style of life' as a fundamental component of status groups.

If some classical sociological authorities of the mid- and late nineteenth century showed a concern with the quality and meaning of social relationships, others were more interested in the properties of large-scale structures. Most obviously, Karl Marx's theory of historical materialism, which attributed human agency to the rather remote and abstract relationships of the main social classes, paid little or no attention to the intermediate ties that bound individuals to one another. The family was dismissed as, at best, a shell that permitted reproduction, at worst, as a microcosm of ownership and control. Trade unions and friendly societies, those associational forms developed by craft and industrial workers to accommodate their interests within a risky and unstable labour market, were seen by Marx and Engels as protective devices by which the aristocracy of labour secured its privileged place within the wider working class, thereby weakening the struggle against the dominant bourgeoisie. Yet if Marxism saw order – or capitalist order at least – as problematic, it was also concerned with the basis of solidarity. If solidarity among the owners of the means of production could be taken as a given, since it merely reflected their desire to maintain their own domination, Marxist theory gave rise to a variety of attempts to explain the strength (or weakness) of solidarity among the oppressed. Marx, in particular, sought to distinguish between what he called a class 'in itself', defined by its objective economic circumstances, and a class 'for itself', whose members were subjectively aware of their common situation and determined to do something about it. From Lenin and Trostky onwards, this distinction stood at the centre of Marxist analyses of the class struggle, particularly in view of the persistent failure of the workers to unite spontaneously against their common class enemy for more than a fleeting historical moment.

A preoccupation with the quality of relationships, and their association with shared values, pervaded classical sociological theory. Perhaps this is unsurprising, for sociology as a discipline emerged as an attempt to explain the origins and nature of social order. Above all, the classical writers were concerned with understanding how humans created stable social structures and patterns of behaviour in a world where urbanisation, industrialisation and scientific rationality had eroded, as it seemed to them, the traditional bases of order: habit, faith and unthinking obedience. Yet in general, classical social theory was not particularly concerned with the areas that are denoted by the concept of social capital, at least in any detail. Although interaction might be treated as an element in social order, or as part of a wider social structure, the questions addressed by the classical theorists are rather different from those tackled by today's social capital researchers. While it is possible to fit theories of social capital into a broadly Marxist, Durkheimian or Weberian perspective on social order, the concept brings a new focus and introduces new questions. The idea of social capital draws attention to the links between the micro-level of individual experiences and everyday activity and the meso-level of institutions, associations and community. Moreover, by defining connections as a form of capital, the concept points broadly towards a set of explanations that can link the micro-, meso- and macro-levels together.

INTEREST IN SOCIAL CAPITAL

Although the power of social capital has been well recognised in daily life for a long time, as a social science concept it has emerged to prominence in relatively recent years. It has attracted attention for a number of reasons. In part, it represents a reaction against what is now seen as the excessive individualism of policy-makers (and voters) in the Reaganite and Thatcherite years. When Margaret Thatcher famously proclaimed, during an interview, that 'There is no such thing as society', many took this quite literally as an exhortation to unbridled individualism. Subsequently, Mrs Thatcher tried to explain that she had simply been arguing that society was a rather abstract notion, and she preferred instead to dwell on the needs of families, individuals and local communities (Thatcher 1993: 626–7), but no one seems to have believed her. Even though the original interview suggests that her explanation was entirely plausible, the more individualistic interpretation had already taken root. In these circumstances, new ideas about the rediscovery of the social appealed to a wider public, as well as to the policy community.

Ideas about social capital are also brought to the fore by recent changes in social behaviour and relationships. Lamentation over the decline of community has become a leitmotif of contemporary journalism. Let me consider just one example among many, which is distinctive only in that it comes from a former editor of *Marxism Today*, fresh on his return from four years in the dynamic environment of Hong Kong, rather than from a backward-looking advocate of traditional values hankering after a lost world of Victorian stability. Looking around Europe, Martin Jacques finds himself dismayed by the erosion of relationships by rampant individualism and the

values of the market. Ours, he complains, is 'a world of increasing imper-
manence, transience and ephemerality, where little or nothing is forever,
and individual gratification is the highest priority'. For many, marriage
has become a short-term arrangement or even something to be avoided,
while having children has become a rarity. Jacques blames what he calls 'the
balkanisation of society' for such ills as a low birth rate and a faltering and
broken process of socialisation of the young, and fears that there are 'dark
times ahead' (Jacques 2002: 24).

Journalistic hyperbole aside, it does seem that in western societies at
least, patterns of interaction are changing. Informalisation of interpersonal
relationships, the continuing erosion of habit and custom as the basis of
human behaviour, the growing division of labour, the blurring of boundaries
between public and private, and the explosion of new means of communication have drawn attention to the ways in which social order is maintained.
The boundaries and contexts of special relationships are no longer explained
or maintained by reference to rigid and formalised codes; to an increasing
extent, they can be chosen, and also given up. We do not need to buy into
the whole postmodernist package to accept that identity and subjectivity
are not unified and given but are open to negotiation and indeterminacy,
even where they are inflected by such inherited attributes as ethnicity
or gender. Neither should we forget that institutionalised roles and relationships still demonstrate a remarkable degree of persistence, of course, as can
be seen at their starkest in the continued inequalities of class and gender.

Social capital has also benefited from the cultural turn in the social
sciences. Along with a marked rise in the attention given to the cultural
aspects of social behaviour, there has been a remarkable growth of interest
in what might be called the micro-level of individual behaviour and
experience. A remarkable number of eminent social scientists have looked
closely at intimacy and trust, to take two examples close to the heart of
social capital (Beck and Beck-Gernsheim 1994; Giddens 1991; Jamieson
1998; Luhmann 1988; Misztal 1996; Sztompka 1999). While most of these
writers have said little about social capital as such (with the exceptions of
Misztal and Stompka), their preoccupations do reflect a concern with the
precise texture of day-to-day interaction and the quality of interpersonal
relationships. This general context of intellectual concern provides a backdrop for the sharp rise of interest among social scientists, in particular, in
social capital.

Finally, social capital has acquired an uneasy relationship with economics.
It has clear parallels with the notion of human capital, which originally

emerged in economics during the 1960s, and denotes the economic value to firms, individuals and the wider public of such attributes as skill, knowledge and good health. In his influential account of school performance in American cities, James Coleman developed the concept of social capital as a way of integrating social theory with economic theory, claiming that social capital and human capital are generally complementary (Coleman 1988–9). Important official bodies like the World Bank and the Organisation for Economic Co-operation and Development have tended to share this view (OECD 2001a, 2001b; World Bank 2001). In a recent report on *The Well-being of Nations*, for example, the OECD argued for 'strong complementarity' between human capital and social capital, with each feeding the other in mutually beneficial ways (OECD 2001b; 13). However, Schuller prefers to see social capital as offering an alternative to the concept of human capital, emphasising the collective where the latter sees only individuals pursuing their self-interests (Schuller 2000). Others have even argued that the notion of social capital represents a colonisation of the social sciences by economists who recognise the limitations of too individualistic a view of human behaviour (Fine 2000). Conceivably, the reverse is equally likely: that is, social capital might be seen as an attempt by sociologists to appropriate one of the core ideas of economics, and apply it to build a bridgehead into their neighbouring (and senior) discipline. My own view is that there is probably some truth in the second view, and that interest in social capital represents an attempt to modify the traditional focus of economists on individual behaviour, by stressing the social basis of peoples' decisions.

AIMS OF THE BOOK

My chief aim in this book is to offer an introduction to the debate over social capital and suggest ways in which the discussion might be taken further in the future. The debate is in some ways a difficult one to summarise, as it crosses a number of scholarly disciplines. While the debate is probably most developed in sociology, the concept has been widely discussed by economists and political scientists, and has attracted attention among some historians, educationalists and feminists as well as specialists in social policy and urban policy. Policy-makers have also shown interest in social capital. Its scope for policy purposes currently encompasses economic development, health promotion, technological development and business innovation, poverty reduction, social inclusion and crime reduction.

The book starts by examining in some detail the ideas of three academics whose work has breathed life into the concept. Pierre Bourdieu, James Coleman and Robert Putnam have all come at the idea from very different backgrounds, and they adopt radically divergent views of the concept. All emphasise the power of networks, though, and the following chapter (Chapter 2) reviews empirical studies of the impact of social capital in such fields as education, health and crime. Most of these studies have concluded that social capital has a generally positive influence; however, the third chapter looks at social capital's darker side, and considers research evidence of its negative impact. Chapter 4 looks at the ways in which current social trends are reshaping social capital (and vice versa), and particularly examines Robert Putnam's claim that these tendencies are depleting our stocks of connectedness. I then review attempts to draw lessons for policy and practice from the debate over social capital. The book concludes with a few brief remarks on the concept's standing in the light of the debates and evidence reviewed here. For what it is worth, my view is that there is plenty of life left in the idea of social capital, and that we are on the verge of a significant explosion in its use by social scientists, policy-makers and the wider public. What remains open is the direction which these developments take, and this depends at least in part on further refinement in the concept, and greater care in its use for explanatory purposes.

1

FROM METAPHOR TO CONCEPT

People's relationships matter greatly to them, as individuals. From a sociological perspective, it could be said that we are, at least partly, defined by whom we know. More broadly, though, bonds between people also serve as central building blocks of the larger social edifice. Of course, this is not a new idea. On the contrary, it was already present when the discipline of sociology was founded. Emile Durkheim, widely acknowledged as a central founding figure in nineteenth-century sociological thought, was particularly interested in the way that people's social ties served as the thread from which a wider society wove itself together. He drew a sharp contrast between the 'mechanical solidarity' of pre-modern societies, where obedience to authority derived from habit and social bonds arose on the basis of similarities in status and routines, and the 'organic solidarity' of the mobile, highly differentiated social systems of modernity. Despite the number, range, complexity and transience that characterise modern social connections, Durkheim noted that society nevertheless

> does not become a jumble of juxtaposed atoms. . . . Rather the members are united by ties which extend deeper and far beyond the short moments during which the exchange is made.
>
> (Durkheim 1933: 226)

So the idea of social ties as contributing to the wider functioning of the community was well established long before the present debate began.

The central idea of social capital is that social networks are a valuable asset. Networks provide a basis for social cohesion because they enable people to cooperate with one another – and not just with people they know directly – for mutual advantage. Initially, the idea of describing social ties as a form of capital was simply a metaphor. According to Robert Putnam, it was invented at least six times during the course of the twentieth century, each time to suggest that using connections to cooperate helped people to improve their lives (Putnam 2000: 19; Woolcock 1998). Strictly speaking, the metaphor implies that connections can be profitable; like any other form of capital, you can invest in it, and you can expect a decent return on your investment. No contemporary social scientists use the term in such a simplistic manner, and it originated as a loose analogy with economic capital, rather than in an ambitious attempt to provide an accountant's balance-sheet for people's social networks. Nevertheless, it is significant that it is a term from economics that has been developed, and that has won such an attentive and wide-ranging audience.

In economic thought, the term 'capital' originally meant an accumulated sum of money, which could be invested in the hope of a profitable return in the future. This is still probably what most people think of if they ever use the term. The concept of 'physical capital', which was introduced to describe the role of machinery and buildings in increasing the productivity of economic activities, followed later. Only in the 1960s was the idea of capital expanded to cover people and their capacities. Initially developed by Theodore Schultz (1961) and then by Becker (1964), the concept behind human capital was that it could be used as a tool that could help the economist measure the value of workers' skills. For Schultz and Becker, labour was much like any other factor of production. It could be more or less productive, and it became more productive as a result of careful investment in, for example, education or health care. So far, then, the various capitals were largely thought of in strictly economic terms; their value was measurable, their worth could be added up and compared, the relationship between inputs and outputs was a direct one, and any changes in value could be accounted for in terms of a common currency. Social contacts are not easily reduced to a simple set of common denominators, and much of the debate about it has taken place outside the discipline of economics, among social thinkers, political scientists, educationalists and historians. Why, and how, has the metaphor developed into a social science concept in this way?

There is a growing consensus that three leading figures have made seminal contributions. Most of this chapter is concerned with the debate that has emerged since the 1980s, and particularly with the profoundly influential writing of Pierre Bourdieu, James Coleman and Robert Putnam. Bourdieu developed the concept of social capital during the 1970s and 1980s, but it attracted much less attention than other areas of his social theory. The subsequent debate was conducted largely in the United States, where James Coleman's attempted fusion of sociology and economics under the banner of rational action theory influenced both social scientists and policy-makers. The concept's current prominence, though, owes much to the work of Robert Putnam, which has attracted a wider publicity. Bob Edwards and Michael Foley have described these writers as representing three 'relatively distinct tributaries' in the literature on social capital (Foley and Edwards 1999: 142), and there are certainly important differences between them, as I show below. In brief, Bourdieu shares with Marxism a concern with questions of unequal access to resources and the maintenance of power; Coleman takes as his starting point the idea of individuals acting rationally in pursuit of their own interests; Putnam has inherited and developed the idea of association and civic activity as a basis of social integration and well-being. Despite these differences, all three consider that social capital consists of personal connections and interpersonal interaction, together with the shared sets of values that are associated with these contacts.

BOURDIEU

Pierre Bourdieu came slowly to the concept of social capital. While Coleman and Putnam were working in a North American tradition of social and political thought, Bourdieu was very much a European sociologist, interested in the persistence of social class and other entrenched forms of inequality. Initially, his stance emerged through his attempt to create a cultural anthropology of social reproduction. In his studies of Algerian tribespeople during the 1960s, Bourdieu described the dynamic development of structured sets of values and ways of thinking as forming what he called 'the habitus', which provided a bridge between subjective agency and objective position. In developing his view of the habitus, Bourdieu emphasised that groups were able to use cultural symbols as marks of distinction, both signalling and constituting their position in the social structure. He gave force to this view by using the metaphor of 'cultural capital', pointing to the way that groups traded on the fact that some types of cultural taste enjoy more status than others. The ability to enjoy Bach, for example, was not a sign of intrinsic superiority but coinage in the cultural currency used by a particular social group in order to maintain superiority over other groups. Moreover, Bourdieu emphasised repeatedly, people's ownership of cultural capital did not just mirror their resources of financial capital. Shaped by family circumstances and school tuition, cultural capital can to some extent operate independently of monetary holdings, and even compensate for lack of money as part of an individual's or a group's strategy to pursue power and status (Jenkins 1992; Robbins 2000).

Bourdieu's early writing on social capital was, then, part of a wider analysis of the diverse foundations of social order. Bourdieu saw the positions of agents in the social field as determined by the amount and weight of their relative capitals, and by the particular strategies that they adopted to pursue their goals. In an interview broadcast on German television in 1987, Bourdieu compared the 'social field' to a casino: we gamble not only with the black chips that represent our economic capital, but also with the blue chips of our cultural capital and the red chips of our social capital (Alheit 1996). These various capitals might not always be substituted for one another, but in combination they may in turn breed new capital (Bourdieu and Passeron 1977).

Bourdieu's definition of these terms varied considerably in depth, with by far the greatest attention going to the concept of cultural capital. In his monumental study of taste and distinction among the French middle class, which draws on a vast battery of empirical indicators of cultural capital, he furnished only one indicator of social capital: membership of golf clubs, which he held to be helpful in oiling the wheels of business life (Bourdieu 1984: 291). Bourdieu published one brief separate outline of his thinking on social capital, which he described with some modesty as 'provisional jottings' (Bourdieu 1980). Subsequently, he attempted to operationalise the concept in further work on social reproduction, such as the monumental empirical study of French high culture (Bourdieu 1984), and in his critique of what he portrayed as the conformity and mediocrity of the French university system (Bourdieu 1988).

In a discussion first published in 1973 of the ways in which members of professional groups secure their position (and that of their children), Bourdieu initially defined social capital as a

   capital of social relationships which will provide, if necessary, useful
   'supports': a capital of honourability and respectability which is often

indispensable if one desires to attract clients in socially important positions, and which may serve as currency, for instance in a political career.

(Bourdieu 1977: 503)

He subsequently refined this position, concluding with the following statement:

Social capital is the sum of resources, actual or virtual, that accrue to an individual or a group by virtue of possessing a durable network of more or less institutionalised relationships of mutual acquaintance and recognition.

(Bourdieu and Wacquant 1992: 119)

Bourdieu also noted that in order that their social capital could maintain its value, individuals had to work at it.

Bourdieu's early comments led to a longer sketch, published in 1980 as 'provisional notes' on social capital, a title that seemed to promise fuller treatment in the future (Bourdieu 1980). At this stage, as has been said, Bourdieu largely treated the concept as an adjunct to or even a dimension of cultural capital (Robbins 2000: 36). In the event, Bourdieu merely reproduced his 'notes' with minor additions and even more minor omissions a year later as part of a chapter on economic, cultural and social capital in a German collection on social inequality, and five years later as a paper on 'the forms of capital' in an English language collection (Bourdieu 1981: 1986). Although he continued to use the concept, in both its scientific and normative dimensions, he did not revisit its theoretical underpinnings.

To understand Bourdieu's thinking on social capital, we need to remember that his main concern was and is the understanding of social hierarchy. In many ways, he was engaging with a body of ideas that was deeply influenced by Marxist sociology. He thought that 'economic capital is at the root of all other types of capital' (Bourdieu 1986: 252), and he was interested in the ways that it could be combined with other forms of capital to create and reproduce inequality. For Bourdieu, inequality was to be explained by the production and reproduction of capital. He reminded readers that capital 'is accumulated labor' which 'takes time to accumulate'. But to see capital solely in economic terms was insufficient. Certainly economic exchanges are geared towards profit, and are therefore pursued out of self-interest. Yet Bourdieu challenged the conventional view that immaterial exchanges – the universe of the artist, or that of love and marriage – were somehow to be respected as 'disinterested' (Bourdieu 1986: 421–2). Both cultural capital and social capital should be treated as assets, representing the product of accumulated labour.

It was impossible, Bourdieu argued, to understand the social world without acknowledging the role of 'capital in all its forms, and not solely in the one form recognised by economic theory' (Bourdieu 1986: 422). He had initially adopted the concept of cultural capital in order to explain the unequal academic achievement of children from different social classes and from different groups within social classes. By pursuing appropriate 'cultural investment strategies' within the family, some social groups were able to ensure that their children optimised the yield from education. In some respects, he argued, the transmission of cultural capital represented the most effective form of hereditary transmission of capital, because it went largely unhidden and therefore was less readily subject to control, whereas the inheritance of economic wealth might be reined by taxation (Bourdieu and Passeron 1977).

Bourdieu brought the same general approach to his account of social capital. In his 'provisional notes', Bourdieu announced that the notion of social capital was the 'sole means' of describing the 'principle of the social assets' which was visible where

> different individuals obtain a very unequal return on a more or less equivalent capital (economic or cultural) according to the extent to which they are able to mobilise by proxy the capital of a group (family, old pupils of elite schools, select club, nobility, etc.).
>
> (Bourdieu 1980: 2)

Characteristically, then, social capital functions to reproduce inequality, but does so partly independently of economic and cultural capital, from which it is nevertheless inseparable. In so far as different forms of capital are not convertible, or more precisely reducible to economic capital, this is because of the differing extent to which they 'disguise the economic aspect'. The more transparent the economic value, the greater the convertibility, but the lower its validity as a source of social differentiation (Bourdieu 1986: 253–4). Rather than convertibility, Bourdieu was interested in the ways that different types of capital together distinguished 'the major classes of conditions of existence'; and, within each of these classes, gave rise to 'secondary differences' on the basis of 'different distributions of their total capital among the different kinds of capital' (Bourdieu 1986: 114).

For Bourdieu, the density and durability of ties were both vital: social capital represented an 'aggregate of the actual or potential resources which are linked to possession of a durable network' (Bourdieu 1980: 2; 1986: 248). He also acknowledged that the value of an individual's ties (or 'volume of social capital possessed by a given agent') depends on the number of connections they can mobilise and the volume of capital (cultural, social and economic) possessed by each connection (Bourdieu 1980: 2; 1986: 249). Bourdieu illustrated the interplay between connections and cultural or financial capital with the example of members of professions, such as lawyers or doctors, who exploit their social capital – namely, 'a capital of social connections, honourability and respectability' – to win the confidence of a clientele in high society, or even make a career in politics (Bourdieu 1984: 122). By contrast, those who rely primarily on their educational qualifications are, he suggests, the most vulnerable in the event of 'credential deflation', not only because they lack connections but also because their weak cultural capital reduces their knowledge about fluctuations in the market for credentials (Bourdieu 1984: 142).

In keeping with his view of capital as the product of accumulated labour, Bourdieu emphasised that connections require work. Solidarity within networks is only possible because membership gives rise to profits, both material and symbolic. Their maintenance therefore requires 'investment strategies, individual or collective' aimed at transforming contingent relationships, such as those of neighbourhood or workplace or even kinship, into 'social relationships that are directly usable in the short or long term'; for these to be effective over the long term, they must involve 'durable obligations subjectively felt' (Bourdieu 1980: 2; 1986: 249). As befits his anthropological concerns, Bourdieu cites the example of gift exchanges: 'the endeavour to personalise a gift' transforms both its purely monetary value and therefore its broader meeting, thus becoming 'a solid investment, the profits of which will appear, in the long run, in monetary or other form' (Bourdieu 1986: 253), with the act of investment taking the form of an 'unceasing effort of sociability' (Bourdieu 1986: 250).

Some British social scientists have claimed that Bourdieu's theory is the most theoretically coherent and persuasive sociological approach to the concept (Fine 2000: 53–64; Warde and Tampubolon 2002: 157). Yet in key respects, Bourdieu's theory remains vulnerable to many of the criticisms levelled at the Marxism that he sought to leave behind. He certainly views social capital as the exclusive property of elites, designed to secure their relative position. His only explanation for relations of affect is that these lend durability to the exchange; he therefore does not allow for the simple fact that some people like (and dislike) each other more than others, even though they may move in the same cultural world and share the same attitudes. He perhaps overemphasises the role of social capital based on kinship. And despite his concern to acknowledge agency, in general his theory appears to be rooted in a relatively static model of social hierarchy.

Bourdieu certainly acknowledges the decline of primordial forms of social organisation in Western countries. For example, he claims that as families lose collective control over some forms of exchange (the marriage choices of their offspring, for example), so new institutions take their place (Bourdieu lists dances, cruises, soirées, receptions and chic sports as examples (1980: 3)) which are designed to favour legitimate exchanges and exclude illegitimate ones. Yet even this example shows that his theory is ill-suited to deal with the more open and loose social relations of late modernity. Cruises, dinner parties, Bach and chic sports are hardly the distinctive badges of today's elites.

For most of Bourdieu's professional life, French social theory was at the heart of European sociological concerns, and Bourdieu held strong views on the merits of his academic peers. During the 1960s and 1970s, much French debate on social inequality took place under the shadow of two dominant intellectual traditions: Marxism, in both its humanist and structuralist variations and social Catholicism, with its organicist model of the social order in which disparities between rich and poor were inseparable from human fate, to be counterbalanced by mutual obligations and rights towards one another. By using the language of multiple capitals, Bourdieu was deliberately marking out his own theoretical territory in opposition to both dominant theories of Marxism. Applying the language of capital to culture and taste or to networks and contacts was itself a strike for materialism against what he saw as the sentimental humanism of the existentialists. Opposing the structuralist Marxism associated with the dense and difficult work of Louis Althusser (Althusser 1977), Bourdieu argued that social life 'is not to be reduced to a discontinuous series of instantaneous mechanical equilibria between agents who are treated as interchangeable particles' (Bourdieu 1986: 241; see also Robbins 2000: 45–9). Yet although he was sharply critical of French Marxism, Bourdieu was clearly not enamoured of conservative social theory, which tended to take inequality as an inescapable part of the human condition, but rather acknowledged openly the influence of Marxist thinking on his highly distinctive approach. Neither was he impressed by the claims of poststructuralism with its emphasis on discourse theory, which he claimed 'reduced social exchanges to phenomena of communication and ignores the brutal fact of universal reducibility to economics' (Bourdieu 1986: 253). In the end, Bourdieu saw his own contribution as the development of an approach that was capable of reconciling structuralist accounts of inequality with constructivist understandings of human agency (Ritzer 1996: 537). This placed him at the crossroads of two central highways in European sociological thought. It is thus all the more remarkable that his work on social capital has been virtually ignored by Coleman and Putnam, as well as by many social scientists who draw selectively on Bourdieu's work on cultural capital.

Yet if Bourdieu's contribution is undeniable, neither is it without flaws. First, like Coleman and Putnam, he represents social capital as largely benign, at least for those who possess high volumes of it. Generally, he shows little interest in social capital's 'dark side', largely because his theory is concerned precisely with the ways in which some groups manipulate their connections in their own interests. His use of the term 'capital' is intended to demystify the humanistic view of social connections, drawing attention to the ways in which they function as an investment strategy. He certainly allows for the possibility of 'embezzlement or misappropriation' of social capital, particularly among those who are allowed to represent institutionalised social capital. Examples of delegated social capital include the paterfamilias who is entitled to speak on behalf of the family, or the aristocrat who benefits from the institutionalised connections of the nobility (Bourdieu 1986: 251). Yet these are simply social capital's counterparts of criminal embezzlers in respect of economic capital. If there is a normative dimension to Bourdieu's theory, then, it is presumably that social capital generally functions to mask the naked profit-seeking of its holders, and is therefore inimical with the open democratic society that he espoused in his journalism and political activism. While his concern for inequality and power are an invaluable corrective to Putnam and Coleman (as we shall see), his one-sided emphasis on the merits of social capital for its holders is a decided weakness.

Bourdieu also tends towards a view of social capital that seems slightly old fashioned and individualistic. As in so many other areas, his fieldwork came largely from studies of the French haute bourgeoisie during the 1960s and early 1970s. His view of the family as subservient to the father smacks somewhat of its time, as does the cachet associated with an appreciation of Bach or jazz in the cultural field. There is little space for collective actors in this view; connections are cultivated by individuals in order to maintain their superiority, and associational life is therefore simply a means to an end. Yet it is also possible to see social capital as a property of groups, and even as quintessentially a product of collective interaction. Furthermore, Bourdieu really thought that social capital was an asset of the privileged and a means of maintaining their superiority. There was no place in his theory for the possibility that other, less privileged individuals and groups might also find benefit in their social ties. Nevertheless, Bourdieu is an important figure in the transition of social capital from being a metaphor to becoming concept. In particular, his analysis of the general logic of social capital and its accumulation, as well as of its interplay with other forms of capital and their accumulation, stands independently of the particular evidence that he provided in respect of the bases of social capital in 1960s France. His contribution therefore deserves closer attention than it has received so far.

COLEMAN

James Coleman, an eminent American sociologist who had considerable influence on the study of education, has had a much wider influence so far than Bourdieu. In a series of investigations of educational attainment in American ghettos, Coleman was able to show that social capital was not limited to the powerful, but could also convey real benefits to poor and marginalised communities. Social capital, according to Coleman, represents a resource because it involves the expectation of reciprocity, and goes beyond any given individual to involve wider networks whose relationships are governed by a high degree of trust and shared values. James Coleman's impact on the concept's development has been far-reaching, particularly in the English-speaking world. In part, this reflects the conceptual clarity and erudition which he brought to what had previously been a somewhat under-theorised notion, if it was known at all to an English-speaking audience. In part, it reflects Coleman's general standing in the social sciences: by the time of his death in 1995 he was one of the most respected and widely debated social theorists in the United States. Like Bourdieu, his work is extensive in its methodological and thematic scope, and has attracted its fair share of controversy. The place of social capital in Coleman's work occupies space within a wider attempt to grapple with the basis of social order, witnessed most dramatically in his monumental late study, *Foundations of Social Theory* (Coleman 1994).

More generally, Coleman was seeking to develop an inter-disciplinary social science that could draw on both economics and sociology. Coleman was particularly influenced by the work of Gary Becker, who like himself was employed at the University of Chicago. Becker's work on human capital, which applied the principles of economics to the study of education, the family, health and discrimination, used the framework of rational choice theory (Becker 1964). Coleman has been rightly claimed as the main moving force behind the rise of rational choice theory in contemporary sociology (Ritzer 1996: 427), and it was within this intellectual framework that he sought to place his conception of social capital. Rational choice (or rational action) theory shares with classical economics a belief that all behaviour results from individuals pursuing their own interests; social interaction is therefore viewed as a form of exchange. From rational choice theory Coleman developed a broad view of society as an aggregation of social systems of individual behaviour. In order to reveal the principles of social order, Coleman proposed that system-level behaviour must be disaggregated into a grasp of individuals' preferences and their actions.

Rational choice sociology assumes a highly individualistic model of human behaviour, with each person automatically doing what will serve their own interests, regardless of the fate of others. The concept of social capital was for Coleman a means of explaining how people manage to cooperate. One example of how this works, much favoured by rational choice theorists, come from game theory. In the mind-game known as the prisoner's dilemma, two individuals are kept in separate cells, then told that the first to inform will receive favourable treatment; the dilemma is whether to keep silent, in the hope that no other evidence exists to prove guilt, and receive no punishment at all if the second player behaves similarly; or confess and receive a reduced punishment. Rational choice theory predicts that the second option will be chosen over the first, since each prisoner knows that the other is likely to confess when faced with the same choice. Nor is the example limited to game theory alone. A similar challenge exists in economic theory more widely in accounting for collective action. For example, employers may choose to behave as free riders when it comes to paying for training; rather than investing in the future skills of their employees, employers may calculate that it is in their interests to hire workers that someone else has trained. In both cases, rational choice theory predicts that each individual will follow their own best interests, even when cooperation might pay better dividends in the long run. Yet in the world outside, and even in departments of economics, people still cooperate.

So, as Barbara Misztal puts it, rational choice theorists constantly face the task of showing that cooperation is consistent with the 'postulates of individualism and self-interest' (Misztal 2000: 109). Social capital seems to have provided Coleman with a resolution of the problem of why human choose to cooperate, even when their immediate interests seem best served by competition. In Coleman's hands, social capital worked in a way that was broadly comparable to, and congruent with, the role of the 'invisible hand' of the market in classical economic theory (Heinze and Strünck 2000: 179).

Like Bourdieu, Coleman's interest in social capital emerged from attempts to explain relationships between social inequality and academic achievement in schools. In *Adolescent Society* (Coleman 1961), Coleman reported the findings of a study of high school students in Chicago, showing that peer group influences (including disapproval) were more likely to shape teenagers' views than those of responsible adults such as parents and teachers. During the mid-1960s, Coleman was asked to direct a major survey of educational achievement and opportunity among six ethnic groups. This piece of research, mandated by an Act of Congress and overseen by the United States Office of Education, has been described as 'a watershed in social science research' (Heckman and Neal 1996: 84), and it became known as the 'Coleman Report'. Drawing on a comprehensive inventory of the inputs and outputs of public education, but with a hitherto unprecedented stress on outputs, Coleman's study confirmed that family and community background characteristics tended to outweigh factors related to the nature of the school itself (Coleman *et al.* 1966). Later, Coleman ruefully reflected that many of the report's original readers had concluded that schools themselves counted for little in comparison with peer group influences, leading to the espousal of bussing and other strategies designed to enforce racial integration in schools, strategies that ultimately had the opposite effects from those intended, in that forced bussing led to 'white flight' from inner city suburbs and increased residential segregation (Coleman 1990: 69–74).

Subsequently, Coleman led a series of empirical studies of achievement in private schools compared with public schools. Using details of family background and cognitive achievement scores for some 50,000 high school sophomores and seniors, Coleman and his collaborators initially reported that pupils tended to perform better at Catholic schools and schools with other religious affiliations even when other factors, such as social class and ethnicity, were taken into account (Coleman *et al.* 1982). A follow-up longitudinal study provided additional evidence on the performance of pupils in Catholic schools, and also showed that these tended to have lower absenteeism and drop-out rates than among pupils of comparable backgrounds and ability in state schools. The findings were particularly striking for pupils from the most disadvantaged socio-economic and ethnic backgrounds, where families had least to contribute to help their children's cognitive development (Hoffer *et al.* 1985; Coleman and Hoffer 1987). Coleman argued that the most important factor in explaining this pattern was the impact of community norms upon parents and pupils, which functioned to endorse teachers' expectations, and he concluded that communities were therefore a source of social capital that could offset some of the impact of social and economic disadvantage within the family (Coleman and Hoffer 1987). Thus Coleman introduced social capital as a post hoc concept, which he had developed partly in order to explain findings that appeared to fit badly into the existing theoretical model (Baron *et al.* 2000: 6). Subsequently, though, he went on to provide a systematic sketch of the concept that has acquired considerable influence over other writers in the social sciences.

Coleman elaborated his definition of social capital in a much-cited paper whose central preoccupation – the relationship between social capital and human capital – reflected his concern with a synthesis of sociology with economics (Coleman 1988–9). His argument was centrally concerned with identifying the contribution of social capital to the development of human capital. Coleman was concerned less with evaluating the relative merits of social capital and human capital as concepts than with distinguishing between them and exploring their interconnection. As he put it somewhat later, rather than being competing concepts, the two pointed to interrelated but separate phenomena that he believed were 'often complementary' (Coleman 1994: 304).

In this paper, he defined social capital as a useful resource available to an actor through his or her social relationships. It comprises a 'variety of entities' that, Coleman surmised, 'all consist of some aspect of social structures, and they facilitate certain actions of actors – whether persons or corporate actors – within the structure' (Coleman 1988–9: 98). Using the conventional economic distinction between public and private goods, Coleman explained how social capital helps understand the problem of collective action. Unlike human and physical capital, which are normally a private good whose ownership and returns reside with individuals, Coleman portrayed social capital quintessentially as a public good that is created by and may benefit not just those whose efforts are required to realise it, but all who are part of a structure (Coleman 1988–9: 116). It therefore demands cooperation between individuals who are nevertheless pursuing their own self-interest.

Coleman provided his most extensive definition of social capital as part of his broader attempt at outlining a general theory of rational choice sociology. Drawing on his earlier paper, Coleman went on to define social capital as

> the set of resources that inhere in family relations and in community social organisation and that are useful for the cognitive or social development of a child or young person. These resources differ for different persons and can constitute an important advantage for children and adolescents in the development of their human capital.
>
> (Coleman 1994: 300)

Elsewhere, he had defined social capital in respect of children's development as

> the norms, the social networks, and the relationships between adults and children that are of value for the child's growing up. Social capital exists within the family, but also outside the family, in the community.
>
> (Coleman 1990: 334)

Social capital is of value, then, not only in the acquisition of credentials but also in both cognitive development and in the evolution of a secure self-identity.

How does social capital achieve this favourable outcome? Remember that Coleman's rational choice sociology assumes that individual actors normally pursue their own self-interest; if they choose to cooperate, it is because it is in their interests to do so. In rational choice theory, cooperation is an exception to the broad rule of solitary, calculating actors who are busy pursuing their own interest. In Coleman's essay on social and human capital, relationships are shown to constitute capital resources by helping to establish obligations and expectations between actors, building the trustworthiness of the social environment, opening channels for information, and setting norms that endorse particular forms of behaviour while imposing sanctions on would-be free-riders (Coleman 1988–9: 102–4). Its creation is facilitated by 'closure' between different networks of actors, by stability, and by a common, shared ideology (Coleman 1994: 104–8, 318–20). Coleman regarded closure – that is, the existence of mutually reinforcing relations between different actors and institutions – as essential in providing not only for the repayment of obligations, but also for the imposition of sanctions. To take one example, it meant that clergy, neighbours and kin acted to reinforce teachers and parents in dissuading young people from playing truant or skipping their homework. Social capital outside the family, he stated, 'exists in the interest, even the intrusiveness, of one adult in the activities of someone else's child' (Coleman 1990: 334).

Coleman's definition of social capital bridged both individual and collective. He certainly viewed social capital as 'a capital asset for the individual', but saw it as built up of 'social structural resources' (Coleman 1994: 302). In determining whether the resources could be called upon in practice, Coleman believed that two 'crucial' elements come into play: both the 'actual extent of obligations held' and 'the level of trustworthiness of the social environment'. These in turn were context-specific, shaped by variations in social structures, including:

> besides the general level of trustworthiness that leads obligations to be repaid, the actual needs that persons have for help, the existence of other sources of aid (such as government welfare agencies), the degree of affluence (which reduces the amount of aid needed from others), cultural differences in the tendency to lend aid and ask for aid, the degree of closure of social networks, the logistics of social contacts.
>
> (Coleman 1994: 306)

This list of factors was not seen by Coleman as exhaustive. Nevertheless, it almost implied that a typology could be constructed of factors favouring the development of social capital, such as network closure or a cultural propensity to request and offer aid, and factors tending to undermine it, such as affluence and welfare systems.

However, from a rational choice perspective, this by no means resolves the underlying problem of explaining why actors should choose to create social capital when they are supposed to be pursuing rationally their own, individual interest. Coleman solved this problem by simply abolishing it: actors did not set out to create social capital as such, rather it arose as an unintended consequence of their pursuit of self-interest. As Coleman put it, social capital arises not because actors make a calculating choice to invest in it, but as 'a by-product of activities engaged in for other purposes' (Coleman 1994: 312). Coleman believed that this distinguished social capital from human or physical capital, both of which arose as a result of deliberate and purposeful choice.

Social capital was, therefore, to be treated as a public rather than private good (Coleman 1994: 312). Yet he still had difficulty in refining his definition to fit with rational choice theory. Whereas Bourdieu could fit his simplified and individualistic notion of social capital into a wider picture of actors who were concerned to reproduce social and economic inequality, Coleman's definition remained both abstract and functionalist. For Coleman,

> Social capital is defined by its function. It is not a single entity, but a variety of different entities having two characteristics in common: they all consist of some aspect of a social structure, and they facilitate certain actions of individuals who are within the structure.
>
> (Coleman 1994: 302)

The question then arises of which particular types of social capital best fulfil this function.

Coleman certainly believed that certain types of social structures were more likely to facilitate individuals' choice of actions than others. In particular, he tended to portray the family as the archetypal cradle of social capital. It is tempting to present this as a result of his interest in children's cognitive development, and it is certainly true that Coleman's clearest definitions of social capital were couched in terms of their value 'for the child's growing up' (Coleman 1990: 334) or 'for the cognitive or social development of a child or young person' (Coleman 1994: 300). More fundamentally, though, Coleman's theoretical framework gave a privileged place to the family as the paramount form of what he called 'primordial' social organisation, which was distinguished by the fact that its origins lay 'in the relationships established by childbirth'. This was contrasted by Coleman with 'constructed' forms of social organisation, which might come together for limited purposes, and represented weaker agencies of social control than primordial forms like the family (Coleman 1991: 1–3). Coleman believed that the erosion of the family and other forms of primordial organisation had led to a transfer of responsibility for primary socialisation to constructed organisations such as schools, leading to a long-term erosion of the 'social capital on which societal functioning has depended' (Coleman 1991: 9). For Coleman, then, kinship in general and the family in particular represented a societal keystone, and he was frankly pessimistic about the prospects for social control rooted in a more artificial set of arrangements.

Even so, Coleman's theoretical framework still allowed for the possibility that some constructed forms of organisation were more likely to promote social capital than others. Here, the archetypal expression of a functional constructed form was the church, which was particularly successful at promoting closure of networks. In an essay that echoes his earlier empirical studies of adolescents, Coleman drew attention to the intergenerational nature of religious ties:

> Religious organisations are among the few remaining organisations in society, beyond the family, that cross generations. Thus they are among the few in which the social capital of an adult community is available to children and youth.
>
> (Coleman 1990: 336)

Yet religious organisations too are waning, and their intellectual message is increasingly heard as one of many competing accounts of human spirituality. Coleman accepts that primordial forms of organisation, with their tight degree of closure, can no longer provide a firm, general basis for societal action among calculating individual actors. Yet he is not entirely satisfied that constructed forms of organisation can provide the normative cohesion and network closure that are required for the assured development of young people.

At first sight, then, Coleman appears to share the old lament over the decline of *Gemeinschaft* or primordial solidarity and its replacement by *Gesellschaft* or constructed solidarity. He also seems to take a rather conservative view of church and family, neither of which retains a central place in underpinning contemporary social life. It has to be said that his view of primordial forms of organisation takes no account of historians' rather more nuanced accounts of family and religion in European and North American societies in past times. Coleman's account therefore appears – like much sociological writing about the past – to rest on a fundamentally ahistorical distinction between 'traditional' and 'modern' or even 'post-modern' social forms. In turn, as Alejandro Portes has pointed out, this emphasis has meant that Coleman tended to overstate the role of close or dense ties, and underestimated the importance of weak or loose ties (Portes 1998: 5). In fact, he often does not acknowledge the immediate and short-term significance of historical processes: his 1961 study makes no mention of the impact of the Second World War on family life, for example (Morrow 1999), nor of its influence on the aspirations and status of African-Americans.

It is instructive to compare Coleman's contribution with Bourdieu's. There are, of course, clear differences between the two. This became apparent in 1989, when Coleman and Bourdieu confronted one another's positions at a conference in Chicago on social theory. While Coleman called for social theorists to engage with 'the problems of constructed social organisation', Bourdieu attempted to defend a humanist view of sociology as a form of reflexive social practice (Robbins 2000: 128–9; Coleman 1991: 8). This general difference in approach can also be found in the two specific accounts of social capital. Bourdieu's treatment of social capital is somewhat circular; in summary, it boils down to the thesis that privileged individuals maintain their position by using their connections with other privileged people. Coleman's view is more nuanced in that he discerns the value of connections for all actors, individual and collective, privileged and disadvantaged. But Coleman's view is also naively optimistic; as a public good, social capital is almost entirely benign in its functions, providing a set of norms and sanctions that allow individuals to cooperate for mutual advantage, and with little or no 'dark side'. Bourdieu's usage of the concept, by contrast, virtually allows only for a dark side for the oppressed, and a bright side for the privileged.

The echoes with Bourdieu are nonetheless fascinating. Most obviously, they share a common concern with social capital as a source of educational achievement. Beyond this, there is also a number of somewhat deeper parallels. Both view social interactions essentially as a form of exchange, although for Coleman this leads to rational choice, while for Bourdieu this constitutes the basis of cultural materialism. Neither pays much heed to affect, to the fact that people like, love or loathe one another – and therefore associate together or avoid each other – for reasons that lie outside the domain of rational calculation. Further, as Piotr Sztompka has remarked, rational choice theory ignores 'basic trust' – a general personal disposition or bias for or against trust, whether generalised or in respect of given connections (Sztompka 1999: 66). So, of course, does Marxist social theory, which assumes that people band together in order to pursue the common interests of their own social class but not because they particularly enjoy one another's company.

Finally, and rather ironically for someone who sought to integrate economic and social theory on the basis of rational choice theory, Coleman is also remarkably negative about individualism. He tends to assume, for instance, that social isolation is inherently damaging and was not found in functioning primordial forms, yet he presents no real argument or evidence in support of either contention (Lindenberg 1996: 303). There are also some apparent inconsistencies in his analysis. For example, it could be argued that his account of social capital's role in building human capital leads logically to the view that individual choice is a poor way of determining the distribution of skills. There are, then, a number of weaknesses in his account, some of which are particularly serious. The strengths must include his ambitious attempt to integrate social capital into a wider theory of the origins of social structures; his recognition that social capital could be an asset for disadvantaged social groups and not solely an instrument of privilege; and his interest in the mechanics of social networks.

PUTNAM

Since the publication of his landmark study, *Bowling Alone* (2000), Robert Putnam has stood out as the most widely recognised proponent of social capital. Whereas Bourdieu and Coleman are best known among the relatively limited worlds of sociology and social theory, Putnam's contribution has leapt the boundaries of his professional field of political science, and reached a far wider public. An essay published in 1995 – based on a paper given to fellow academics at Uppsala in 1994 – attracted the attention of Bill Clinton, and Putnam duly found himself summoned to Camp David. The appearance of *Bowling Alone* was treated as a significant news event. Putnam was interviewed in the broadsheets and on talk shows, and was photographed together with his wife for the pages of *People*. He then embarked on what was almost a world tour, crossing North America and Europe to promote the ideas in his book. A lively speaker, and an eloquent writer, Putnam is characteristically modest about his sudden rise to fame, which he attributes not to 'late-blooming genius, but the simple fact that I had unwittingly articulated an unease that had already begun to form in the minds of many ordinary Americans' (Putnam 2000: 506).

In contrast with the sociologists Coleman and Bourdieu, Putnam's background lies in political science. After working under Ron Inglehart on the relationship between social values and political attitudes, Putnam's first major study concerned the role of civic engagement in generating political stability and economic prosperity, based on fieldwork in Italy. Subsequently, Putnam rapidly turned his attention to the USA, and published a series of papers claiming to demonstrate that there has been a sizeable 'decline' of social capital since the 1940s, which explains the ungovernability of much of urban America. As his own comments on his late fame suggest, this thesis speaks to a long tradition of concern over the state of democracy and community in the USA. This concern can be traced back to the first half of the nineteenth century, and above all to the reception in the US of the writings of Alexis de Tocqueville, the nineteenth-century French author, which have continued to resonate through North American political analysis to the present day.

Reflecting on his travels throughout the United States in 1831, de Tocqueville was initially rather alarmed at what he took to be the near anarchy of the world's first sizeable democracy. Somewhat conservative in his views, de Tocqueville believed that formal equality before the law must tend to produce a society of atomised individuals, which would then lead to despotism. As he travelled, though, he changed his views, discovering in American associational life an unparalleled arena for civic learning:

> In their political associations the Americans, of all conditions, minds, and ages, daily acquire a general taste for association and grow accustomed to the use of it. There they meet together in large numbers, they converse, they listen to one another, and they are mutually stimulated to all sorts of undertakings. They afterwards transfer to civil life the notions they have thus acquired and make them subservient to a thousand purposes.
> (De Tocqueville 1832: Book 2, Ch. VII)

For de Tocqueville, then, associational life was an important foundation of social order in a relatively open, clearly post-aristocratic system. A high level of civic engagement, far from inviting despotism, taught people how to cooperate across civil life; it was the nursery of a democratic society. Putnam's message has found such a wide audience precisely because he suggests that the Tocquevillian foundation stone of American democracy is starting to crumble.

Putnam's first contribution to the debate on social capital came towards the end of a study of regional government in Italy (Putnam 1993a). Drawing on two decades of empirical data collection, Putnam sought to identify and then explain differences between regional administrations in the north and south of Italy. Putnam primarily took an institutional approach to the study, concentrating on the relative performance of public policy actors in north and south, and concluding that the relatively successful institutional performance of the northern regions was due to the mutual interrelationship between government and civil society. He traced the origins of this beneficial civic virtue back to the activities of the early medieval guilds in the largely autonomous, self-regulating city-states of the north. By contrast, he believed that the origins of the stand-off between state and civil society in the south lay in the period of Norman autocracy, which created a culture of mutual suspicion and fear which had stood repeatedly in the way of institutional reform and renewal.

Putnam used the concept of social capital to shed further light on these differences in civic engagement. He defined the term only after presenting a detailed discussion of his evidence of relative institutional performance and levels of civic engagement:

> Social capital here refers to features of social organisation, such as trust, norms and networks, that can improve the efficiency of society by facilitating coordinated actions.
>
> (Putnam 1993a: 167)

More precisely, social capital contributes to collective action by increasing the potential costs to defectors; fostering robust norms of reciprocity; facilitating flows of information, including information on actors' reputations; embodying the successes of past attempts of collaboration; and acting as a template for future cooperation (Putnam 1993a: 173). In his Italian study, though, Putnam's use of social capital was in several respects largely an extension of Coleman's. He certainly paid much more attention than Coleman to the resources that are accrued through loose ties, built up though constructed organisations such as rotating credit associations and singing societies, and took a more limited view than Coleman of the role of church and family.

After publishing his study of Italian political institutions, Putnam switched his focus to his native United States. His scholarly messages were punchy ones, reinforced by titles whose economy and style packed the immediacy of a newspaper headline. The most telling example is probably *Bowling Alone*, a title he gave to both his most recent book and an earlier scholarly paper (Putnam 1995; 2000). The vivid image of a solitary bowler was to capture the journalistic imagination, though as usual this was at the cost of some oversimplification. Putnam's point in using the metaphor was not that Americans travelled on their own to play in isolation, but that they were ever less likely to play in formal teams against regular sets of opponents in organised bowling leagues (as he himself had done in his youth) and more likely to play with a group of family or friends. Putnam's message in his articles throughout the mid-1990s was a consistent one: America's social capital was in a state of long-term decline, and the main culprit in its demise was the rise of television (Putnam 1993b; 1995; 1996).

League bowling served here as a metaphor of a type of associational activity that brings relative strangers together on a routine and frequent basis, helping to build and sustain a wider set of networks and values that foster general reciprocity and trust, and in turn facilitate mutual collaboration.

Putnam's definition of social capital changed little over the 1990s. In 1996, he stated that

> by 'social capital' I mean features of social life – networks, norms and trust – that enable participants to act together more effectively to pursue shared objectives.
>
> (Putnam 1996: 56)

The three primary ingredients here had not changed since 1993; what was new was the identification of 'participants' in particular rather than 'society' as the beneficiaries of social capital (Baron *et al*. 2000: 9). Subsequently, in his landmark book, Putnam argued that

> the core idea of social capital theory is that social networks have value . . . social contacts affect the productivity of individuals and groups.
>
> (Putnam 2000: 18–19)

The term itself he defined as referring

> to connections among individuals – social networks and the norms of reciprocity and trustworthiness that arise from them.
>
> (Putnam 2000: 19)

This formulation seems to mark a refinement of the earlier definition, in that it presented trust (together with reciprocity) as an essential element of the norms that arise from social networks, and thus leaves us with two rather than three primary ingredients, namely networks and norms.

Putnam then introduced a distinction between two basic forms of social capital: bridging (or inclusive) and bonding (or exclusive). Bonding social capital tends to reinforce exclusive identities and maintain homogeneity; bridging social capital tends to bring together people across diverse social divisions. Each form is helpful in meeting different needs. Bonding social capital is good for 'undergirding specific reciprocity and mobilising solidarity', while serving as 'a kind of sociological superglue' in maintaining strong in-group loyalty and reinforcing specific identities. Bridging connections 'are better for linkage to external assets and for information diffusion', and provide a 'sociological WD–40' that can 'generate broader identities and reciprocity' (Putnam 2000: 22–3).

Putnam's theory of social capital, then, shows marked similarities to Durkheimian notions of solidarity. His use of words like 'productivity' and 'effectively' suggest that he sees social capital as functional, but the context makes clear that he is not depicting the calculating individual actor of rational choice theory. Unlike Coleman, Putnam explicitly rejected Tönnies' contrast between organic community (*Gemeinschaft*) and achieved social organisation (*Gesellschaft*), with its conclusion that modernity is the enemy of civility. On the contrary, Putnam argued that his Italian study had shown that 'The least civic areas . . . are precisely the traditional southern villages' (Putnam 1993a: 114). Kinship is less important as a source of solidarity than acquaintanceship and shared membership of secondary associations, which could bring together individuals from quite distinctive and separate small groups (Putnam 1993a: 175). He also argued that 'vertical' bonds might be less helpful than 'horizontal' ties, in that they might undermine the capacity for collective action and tend to create suspicion (Putnam 1993a: 195). But while we may detect similarities with Durkheim, these should not be overplayed. As Barbara Misztal has said, Putnam is a theoretically eclectic writer who draws both on a Durkheimian analysis of mutual bonds and on an emphasis on actors' rationality that comes from rational choice theory (Misztal 2000: 119).

In a manner entirely reminiscent of de Tocqueville, he is clearly also inspired by a straightforward enthusiasm for volunteering and sociability as counterweights to excessive corporate power and social apathy. Certainly Putnam's Italian study was notable for drawing on de Tocqueville, not only as a general intellectual inspiration, but specifically for two of the four indicators that he used to measure civic engagement: associational life and newspaper readership (the other two being electoral turnout and preference voting patterns). He also shares de Tocqueville's enthusiasm for civic associations, but not his fears about the tendency of democratic societies to drift towards despotism. If Putnam has a dystopia, it appears to be rather a society of constant television oglers, typified by political apathy and casual disregard for other people, where crime and poverty go untackled and the prospects of long-term economic prosperity are bleak. In this sense, then, it is only partly accurate to describe Putnam as a neo-Tocquevillean.

The real core of Putnam's study of the USA, however, lies in its meticulous assembly of empirical detail. He presents the evidence for a decline in social capital in America in considerable detail, particularly in *Bowling*

Alone, which systematically analyses a range of statistical data on social trends over the second half of the twentieth century. For his earlier paper, Putnam relied heavily on the widely used General Social Survey (conducted every two years since 1974) and the National Election Studies (conducted every year since 1952), which provided a record of changing attitudes and behaviour in the United States. For his subsequent book, Putnam supplemented these basic sources with a range of other data, including the membership records of a variety of national bodies, from the Elks to labour unions. He also drew on other survey data, most notably the DDB Needham Life Style Surveys (conducted annually since 1975) and the Social and Political Trends survey conducted by the Roper polling organisation between 1973 and October 1994 (Putnam 2000: 415–24).

Of course none of these sources had originally been compiled in order to answer the questions that Putnam was posing. In this respect, his approach adopted the procedures of historians, who invariably make use of data compiled by other people for quite different purposes. In Putnam's case, virtually all the evidence pointed in the same direction. By the late 1880s, urbanisation, immigration and industrialisation had brought America's communal ties to a low point, from which sprang a dense web of voluntary organisations, from the Red Cross to Hadassah to the labour unions. Civic engagement then grew steadily until the Depression, returning to its earlier rates of growth after the United States entered the Second World War. Then from the 1960s, slowly at first, and then with the force of 'a treacherous rip current', Americans 'have been pulled apart from one another and from our communities' (Putnam 2000: 27).

The sheer weight of the accumulated evidence of decline since the 1960s is compelling. It appears, on Putnam's data, to hold true for political participation, associational membership, religious participation, volunteering, charity, work-based socialising, and informal social networks, all of which are considered in detail and shown to have declined more or less in step with one another. Putnam links this pattern with survey data showing that Americans' perceptions of honesty and trustworthiness have declined, from a peak in the mid-1960s. Again, this evidence of attitudinal change is supplemented with data on behavioural change, such as the growing tendency of American drivers to ignore stop signs at intersections (Putnam 2000: 143) and the sharp rise in reported crime. And although Putnam notes some countertrends, such as the growth of small self-help groups and youth volunteering, and the rise of new ways of communicating through the Internet and other technologies, he ultimately concludes that the evidence is 'ambiguous', and certainly does not 'outweigh the many other ways in which most Americans are less connected to our communities than we were two or three decades ago' (Putnam 2000: 180).

Putnam then parades a row of possible causes of this long-term decline, considering each culprit in turn before turning to examine the consequences. He dismisses such candidates as the transformation of family structures and the growth of the welfare state – popular among conservative thinkers – on the grounds that neither appears plausible in the light of his data for the USA, nor are they consistent with patterns elsewhere (particularly Scandinavia). Nor does he accept the left–liberal thesis that declining social capital is caused by racism, and particularly 'white flight' from racially mixed cities to ethnically homogeneous suburbs; this hypothesis fails in the light of evidence that 'the erosion of social capital has affected all races', and that the most connected generations are those who came of age at a time when American society was more segregated and racist than it is today (Putnam 2000: 280). He is less dismissive of another liberal idea, however, namely that declining civic engagement is caused by the growing power of big business. While he notes that market capitalism was equally hegemonic in the USA when civic engagement was at its peak, and therefore cannot provide the main reason for contemporary disconnectedness, he does allow that trends towards globalisation have reduced the civic commitment of business leaders. However, while this may help explain some of the decline, there is no obvious reason why globalisation should influence 'our readiness to attend a church social, or to have friends over for poker' (Putnam 2000: 283).

Ultimately, Putnam fingers four chief culprits. First, sheer busyness and the pressures associated with two-career families have reduced the amount of time and other resources that women in particular can devote to community involvement. However, Putnam regards this as at most a contributory factor, since connectedness and engagement have diminished almost equally for men and women, whether working or not (Putnam 2000: 203). Second, he notes that the residents of large metropolitan areas suffer from what he calls a 'sprawl civic penalty', as they are required to spend increased amounts of time getting around, and their ties tend to be more fragmented (Putnam 2000: 215). However, civic engagement has also decline in small towns and rural areas; like pressures of time and money, Putnam regards urban mobility and sprawl as a contributory factor. The two main culprits, he concludes, are home-based electronic entertainments, above all television; and generational change. Putnam's data suggest that heavy television users have virtually dropped out of civic life and spend little time with friends or even, increasingly, family (he also presents evidence that heavy viewers generally tend to feel unwell, and derive little pleasure from their viewing (Putnam 2000: 240–2)). Finally, though, Putnam notes that age is the only factor which proves an exception to the broad pattern of falling civic engagement. Controlling for variations in educational attainment, Putnam finds that people born in the 1920s belong to nearly twice as many associations as their grandchildren born in the 1960s, are twice as likely to vote, and are almost three times as likely to read a newspaper (Putnam 2000: 254). This 'unusually civic generation', forced into cooperative habits and values by 'the great mid-century global cataclysm' of war and reconstruction, is being inexorably replaced by others who are less civic minded (Putnam 2000: 275).

Putnam then poses the question: so what? Does it matter that America's social capital is in decline? Putnam answers these questions by a number of attempts to investigate the relationship between social capital and such indicators of well-being as education, economic prosperity, health, happiness and democratic engagement. He combines fourteen separate measures of social capital, such as levels of social trust and engagement in civic affairs, into a single Social Capital Index, which he then uses to map levels of social capital for each of the fifty American states. Broadly, these data seem to show that social capital is spread most thinly in the Mississippi Delta, in the heart of the old South; social capital is at its densest in the Mid-West, extending right along the central border with Canada (Putnam 2000: 290–3). Putnam then proceeds to demonstrate that, for a range of indicators of well-being, states such as Mississippi, Alabama and Louisiana tend to perform rather badly, while states such as Minnesota, Iowa, and the New England state of Vermont tend to do rather well. Significantly, given his hypothesis on the role of electronic entertainments, Putnam also shows a very strong correlation between the time spent by children watching TV and ranking on the Social Capital Index (Putnam 2000: 303). Putnam devotes a rather brief chapter to what he calls the 'dark side' of social capital, but contents himself with noting that there may at times be a tension between bridging and bonding capital. He illustrates his argument with reference to the bussing controversy, when African-American children were enrolled at predominantly white schools, and white children enrolled at schools with a predominantly African-American catchment area. However, overwhelmingly, Putnam believes that his evidence points to a powerful positive association between social capital and well-being, and he devotes the final chapters of this massive study to the discussion of policies for creating (or re-creating) social capital.

Putnam's contribution is monumental. His scholarship rests on a wide-ranging knowledge of a variety of sources of evidence. His wider visibility and influence have ensured that his approach has virtually eclipsed those of Coleman and Bourdieu. Needless to say, this high profile has attracted critique as well as praise. His work on Italy has been subjected to scrutiny by historians as well as political scientists, and his work on the United States has always attracted controversy. How well has Putnam's work stood up to the criticisms?

First, a number of writers have asked whether Putnam's evidence stands up to the weight of his thesis. In an early critique, one American writer suggested that Putnam's indicators of engagement were largely 'out of date'; bodies such as the Elks and Red Cross are tied more to the older cities and more fixed gender-based roles; new forms of engagement such as youth soccer are growing because they are geared more to busy, suburbanised ways of life (Lemann 1996: 25–6). More recently, the same critique has been pursued in greater detail (Cohen 1999: 212–19). However, it has to be said that this criticism may have lost some of its force since the publication of *Bowling Alone*, in which Putnam explores some newer forms of association, including youth soccer and the new social movements of the 1970s and 1980s. As noted above, Putnam accepts that the evidence is ambiguous, but insists that on closer inspection the overall pattern of decline is unmistakable. Even growing movements like Greenpeace appear to conform to this pattern; they recruit by direct mail rather than personal persuasion, require less commitment from their members, involve more ephemeral forms of support, and create fewer long-standing personal ties among supporters than did the 'old-fashioned' chapter-or branch-based organisations that they appear to be displacing (Putnam 2000: 158–60).

Of course, this may simply be a case of American exceptionalism. Several writers have noted that Putnam's evidence of declining engagement in the United States has to be set aside contrasting evidence of vibrancy in Western Europe (Rothstein 2001; Hall 1999; Maloney *et al.* 2000a). This is particularly significant, in that European societies closely resemble the USA in patterns of leisure and generational change. We might therefore expect these societies to show similar declines of civic engagement, if Putnam's diagnosis is accurate. It remains to be seen whether Rothstein's and Hall's studies of social capital in Sweden and Britain are any more typical of

Western trends than Putnam's. If they are, then this might suggest that Putnam must revisit his explanation of declining civic engagement in the USA, but it would not undermine his basic diagnosis of decline.

More fundamentally, Putnam has been accused of adopting a 'rather circular' definition of social capital (Misztal 2000: 121). He is also said to lack theoretical precision. He allegedly fails to provide an account of the production and maintenance of social capital (Misztal 2000: 120), and 'takes for granted' the 'causal link that connects trust and a rich network of associations' (Sztompka 1999: 196). Certainly it is true that his theory does not prescribe a particular relationship between the different elements of social capital. His definition, however, is certainly concise. And in *Bowling Alone*, the emphasis is clearly placed upon active participation in networks; 'the norms of reciprocity and trustworthiness that arise from them' (Putnam 2000: 19) are here reduced to the status of powerful subordinate factors.

It has also been alleged that Putnam's conceptual vagueness is associated with too celebratory a tone (Portes 1998: 1). Social capital is not merely benign; in Putnam's hands, it is almost a cure-all for each of society's many ills. For Jean Cohen, there is even a risk that Putnam is playing unintentionally into the hands of those who are seeking to damage the welfare state; she even describes him as a 'neorepublican' (Cohen 1999: 211, 228). But if Cohen is overstating the case, certainly his work is often viewed as compatible with at least some versions of communitarianism (Schuller *et al.* 2000: 10). Thus Misztal believes that Putnam has promoted a 'romanticised image of community', failing to see that networks can foster both trust *and* distrust (Misztal 2000: 121). The extent to which nostalgia influences Putnam can be seen from his invocation of George Bailey, the central character in Frank Capra's *It's a Wonderful Life*, acted by James Stewart. For Putnam, Bailey was among the 'civic heroes' who evoked not mere nostalgia but 'a time when public-spiritedness really did carry more value and when communities really did "work"' (Putnam 2000: 287). Indeed, the film, which was released shortly after the end of the Second World War, is a stunningly successful evocation of community, and the video continues to sell well. I might as well come clean: I enjoy watching it at Christmas myself, and its final scene of community reconciliation still brings tears to my eyes. Ironically, and interestingly in view of Putnam's argument, the film may speak volumes in turn-of-millennium America, but it flopped at the box office in 1948. Only later did *It's a Wonderful Life* acquire the status of a classic. Ironically, rather than celebrating the virtues of community engagement, Capra's emphasis is rather on the heroic individual, standing alone against corporate corruption. So on the count of nostalgia, to use a phrase that Putnam might have adopted, the defendant stands guilty as charged.

Putnam has also come under attack for underestimating the importance of politics. Significantly, while his account of social capital is interdisciplinary, its roots lie in political science. It is curious, then, that one of his weaknesses appears to be an oversocialised view of behaviour. Because he views social capital as generated solely through long-term social and economic processes, there seems to be little scope for human agency in his account. His 1993 study of Italian regional government, which traced civic virtue back to the early medieval period, is a particularly striking example of this approach. At best, it could be said that he views the production of social capital as highly path dependent, in that its present-day condition is ultimately the outcome of a series of long-term historical processes. This is associated with a tendency to overlook the role of the state (Misztal 2000: 120). In Putnam's defence, it could be said that his American studies are perhaps a little less long term than his work on Italy, in that he believes that the collapse of civic engagement has taken at most two generations (Lemann 1996). Political scientists have gone further, suggesting that his view has bent too far towards sociology. One group of British authors has criticised Putnam for 'taking a bottom-up perspective' that emphasises volunteering and 'neglects the role played by political activities and institutions' (Maloney *et al.* 2000b: 803). Lowndes and Wilson similarly criticise Putnam's theory as 'too society-centred, undervaluing state agency and associated political factors' (Lowndes and Wilson 2001: 629).

This understandable attempt to return the focus at least partly to the traditional territory of political scientists – namely institutions and decision-making processes – emphasises that governments are not passive players in this process, but can shape the framework within which citizens decide whether to engage in the public sphere, or stay at home and watch TV. However, the sociological critique of Putnam's neglect of agency is perhaps even more telling. We can only understand withdrawal from engagement if we take it seriously, and understand it as an active choice.

On the topic of social capital, Putnam's has become the dominant voice. Partly this is because of the analytical clarity and detailed historical sweep of his work, particularly *Bowling Alone*. However, he has acknowledged the influence of Coleman's writing, and Coleman in turn was well aware of Bourdieu's contribution. Many of the criticisms made of one writer could equally be made of at least one of the others, and sometimes of all three.

Moreover, there are precursors to all three. While Coleman and Putnam credit the economist Glenn Loury with coining the concept of social capital (Putnam 1993a: 241), its separate elements – networks, participation, shared values, trustworthiness – have all been familiar subjects of scholarly interest for some time. It is therefore helpful to ask what distinctive contribution has been made by Bourdieu, Coleman and Putnam, and where it leaves the debate.

WHAT HAVE THE SOCIAL CAPITAL CLASSICS ADDED?

What does the idea of social capital bring to the analysis of relationships and behaviour? Surely, if the concept does add anything new in analytical terms, it lies in its focus on networks and relationships as a resource. This is how social capital has been conceived by Bourdieu, Coleman and Putnam, but they each did so in different ways. Bourdieu has taken this approach in one direction, seeing social capital as an asset used by elite groups – particularly those who had limited financial capital and/or cultural capital, such as the French nobility – in their jockeying for position. For Coleman, social capital could also serve as a resource for the relatively disadvantaged, but he shared with Bourdieu an emphasis on the asset as something belonging to individuals or families. Putnam has stretched the concept furthest, in seeing it as a resource that functions at societal level. This feature makes Putnam's account vulnerable to the accusation of functionalism, and may help explain his relentless emphasis upon social capital's bright side. If Putnam and Coleman tend to understate the importance of power inequalities in their accounts (Hibbitt *et al.* 2001: 145), Bourdieu is equally guilty of underplaying the importance of social capital to otherwise disadvantaged groups.

For some writers, this very use of a language of capital is inappropriate. Jean Cohen, for instance, maintains that it is entirely wrong, suggesting as it does 'a false analogy between direct interpersonal relations and economic exchanges on the market', whereas interpersonal relationships and trust are 'by definition specific and contextual' (Cohen 1999: 220–1). But this is probably expecting too much of a concept that has not entirely shed the status of a metaphor. Coleman in particular noted what he described as the limited 'fungibility' of social capital, speaking of the way in which social capital may be a positive resource in some contexts but could be useless or even harmful in others (Coleman 1994: 302). But Coleman also noted that this was true of human and physical capital, and Putnam made the same point even more bluntly, pointing out that an aircraft carrier and an egg beater might both appear as physical capital in the accounts, but neither would be much practical use if they were swapped (Putnam 2000: 21).

All three writers might be criticised for the 'gender-blindness' of their work. Feminist critics have noted that much civic engagement is highly gendered (Lowndes 2000), and they have also suggested that Coleman's inherently conservative view of the family has significant consequences for his analytical framework (Blaxter and Hughes 2001). Although Putnam made some effort in *Bowling Alone* to pay specific attention to gender as a factor in the creation and decline of social capital, his comments appear to have been rather impressionistic, and lack the usual detailed basis of evidence that otherwise underpins his argument. For example, when he applies the Yiddish *macher* to describe those who make things happen in the community and *schmoozer* for those who engage in flexible and informal conversation and activities, Putnam asserts that *machers* tend to be 'disproportionately male' while 'informal social connections are much more frequent among women', and then concludes that 'women are more avid social capitalists than men' (Putnam 2000: 94–5). Despite a lengthy footnote devoted to this issue, the evidence basis for this judgement remains unclear. For both Coleman and Bourdieu, gender is largely ignored (Morrow 1999). The obvious question arising from this general reluctance to explore the gender dimension of a clearly gendered practice is whether the concept itself is fundamentally flawed, or whether this is simply a product of a rather traditional approach to the evidence. My own view is somewhat closer to the latter than the former, for reasons explored in Chapter 4.

The three foundational authors may also be criticised for developing a somewhat undifferentiated concept of social capital. Their approaches can be seen as excessively homogenised in at least three ways. First, they largely downplay the negative consequences of social capital. Coleman regards it as almost entirely benevolent; Putnam acknowledges a 'down side', but his treatment of this is cursory; and Bourdieu, who clearly regards social capital as an asset of the most privileged, views it as negative only for the disadvantaged. The negative dimension to social capital is explored further in Chapter 3. Second, the foundational approaches are somewhat ahistorical. Bourdieu is particularly culpable in this respect, tying his conception of social capital to a series of empirical studies that were located in French academia during the 1960s. Coleman and Putnam certainly allow for change over time, but do so in a rather crude form; basically, they allow for the possibility that the volume of social capital may grow or diminish with time (mostly they lament the latter), but not that its components and outcomes may alter, with consequences for all concerned.

Finally, the three foundational definitions do not really distinguish between different types of social capital. Michael Woolcock has made a particularly helpful distinction between:

(a) bonding social capital, which denotes ties between like people in similar situations, such as immediate family, close friends and neighbours;
(b) bridging social capital, which encompasses more distant ties of like persons, such as loose friendships and workmates; and
(c) linking social capital, which reaches out to unlike people in dissimilar situations, such as those who are entirely outside the community, thus enabling members to leverage a far wider range of resources than are available within the community.

(Woolcock 2001: 13–14)

Putnam has recently embraced Woolcock's ideas of bonding and bridging ties, but does not really explore the logical conclusion, which is that different combinations of the three types of social capital will produce different outcomes.

On balance, it seems that Coleman's approach has the greatest potential for producing new insights into social and political behaviour. His view of social capital as a distributed resource may have been what led Robert Putnam to identify Coleman's *Foundations of Social Theory* (1994) as a key influence in his own first full-length treatment of social capital (Putnam 1993a: 241). Putnam's work, while popularising the concept and bringing it to new audiences, has also been clearly rooted in empirical evidence, and this has in turn generated significant new debates as scholars seek to test his ideas and evidence against their own. Bourdieu's usage is somewhat more narrow than Coleman's or Putnam's, but its location within a wider account of the social space could prove fruitful, while his debt to neo-Marxism brings a strong recognition of the connection between social capital and power – something largely ignored by Putnam and Coleman. However, even Coleman's approach requires further refinement. It privileges particular types of social capital, in particular the family, and downplays the role of loose networks and ties. It is not only somewhat normative, but might even be accused of naiveté and optimism. It is insufficiently attentive to conflict and power.

Yet it would be wrong to follow those who believe the concept to be too loose and elastic to have any analytical value. Alejandro Portes has argued that while the concept does call attention to 'real and important phenomena', the time is arriving 'at which social capital comes to be applied to so many events and in so many contexts as to lose any distinct meaning' (Portes 1998: 1, 18). But the same could be said – indeed has been – of virtually any concept in the social sciences, including human capital, power, class and gender. The issue is not whether a concept can be applied loosely, but whether it leads to new insights when applied finely. In drawing our attention to the ways in which networks and shared values function as a resource for people and organisations, the concept of social capital has earned its share of the social scientific limelight.

2

EXPLORING THE POWER OF NETWORKS

The idea of social capital is influencing researchers and thinkers right across the social sciences. Scholars have drawn on the work of Putnam, Coleman and Bourdieu to provide a theoretical framework for examining the impact of people's networks on their life chances. Of course, the concept has also attracted attention among policy-makers and others who are interested in it because of its practical applications. This chapter, though, focuses on the way social capital has been used by scholars working in a range of disciplines, including sociology, politics, economics, health, social work, history, education and criminology. In each of these disciplines, the idea that relationships can serve as a resource has been repeatedly tested in a wide variety of different empirical contexts. Of course, the idea that social networks matter, along with the norms that hold them together, is hardly a novelty. An old British saw holds that 'It isn't what you know but who you know'. As in common sense, so the importance of networking is well established in the social sciences. What the concept of social capital has brought to the debate is, at bottom, an interest in the pay-offs that arise from our relationships.

The idea that social capital returns tangible benefits to its holders is obviously open to testing against evidence. This chapter therefore starts by reviewing the findings of research that has been influenced by the concept, with the aim of seeing how well the theory stands up to empirical scrutiny. Inevitably, the coverage is selective: social capital has had a wide range of application, and inevitably the level of research evidence is variable; moreover, what some readers may see as the central question of civic engagement is dealt with later, in Chapter 4 (see below, pages 96–101). Four themes are discussed in this chapter: education, economic growth, health and crime. To summarise the findings of a wide variety of research, it seems that in general, social capital broadly does what the theorists have claimed: to put it crudely, people who are able to draw on others for support are healthier than those who cannot; they are also happier and wealthier; their children do better at school, and their communities suffer less from anti-social behaviour. This is an impressive list of benefits, but these alone do not answer all the questions that might be posed about the concept. Accordingly, the chapter then explores some other aspects of the way in which the concept has been operationalised. In particular, it tackles two issues that have persistently led to questions about the coherence of the concept. It considers whether trust is an integral element of social capital, or alternatively is one of its by-products, and it asks how far the metaphor of 'capital' is appropriate to the study of human relationships.

SOCIAL CAPITAL AND EDUCATION

Both Bourdieu and Coleman have influenced the sociology of education, and it is with the impact of social capital on education that this review of research begins. Coleman's own work was particularly noteworthy, in that it was grounded in the analysis of large-scale survey data as well as his seminal paper on the contribution of social capital to human capital. As we have already seen, Coleman drew on earlier work which looked at the performance of black children in American secondary schools (see Chapter 1, pages 22–3). His findings attracted considerable attention, at least partly because they were unexpected. Conventionally, sociologists generally expect that those children whose families are socially and economically well-placed will tend to outperform those who come from more disadvantaged backgrounds. Nor are they wrong to do so. Mostly, families' cultural and economic capital are reflected in the human capital – that is, the skills, knowledge and qualifications – of their children. Coleman's research shed light on some of the exceptions to this general rule.

As his findings were both unexpected and controversial, it is not surprising that Coleman's work in particular has accordingly been subjected to detailed scrutiny. In a review of educational research into social capital, Sandra Dika and Kusum Singh note that much of the work conducted between 1990 and 1995 was characterised by a focus on minority ethnic populations (Dika and Singh 2002: 36). Coleman was himself responsible for a number of follow-up studies (Coleman *et al*. 1982; Coleman and Hoffer 1987) on the performance of minorities in private and public schools, confirming the impact of faith-based schools on pupil achievement, and also demonstrating that Catholic schools have substantially lower drop-out rates among students of similar backgrounds and ability levels. Other scholars have undertaken a number of studies designed to test Coleman's propositions, mostly using different data-sets and methods. Generally these have upheld Coleman's findings with regard to both drop-out rates and student achievement, confirming that the gains from Catholic schooling are particularly marked for urban minorities. However, it should be added that more recently, some scholars have criticised Coleman for a failure to consider the effect of parental choices of school upon the performance of their children (Heckman and Neal 1996: 94–6). The evidence of studies that were deliberately designed to test Coleman's propositions is therefore problematic. While the findings are broadly consistent with Coleman's, the possibility remains that the explanation lies at least partly in the decisions made by parents, which means that his sample suffered from an inadvertent selection bias. Moreover, as Dika and Singh point out (2002: 37), a number of the studies did not strictly follow Coleman's definition of social capital, including some which took the view that command of a minority language could itself be seen as a collective resource (e.g. Stanton-Salazar and Dornbusch 1995).

More recent work has generally tended to confirm that social capital seems to be closely associated with educational outcomes. Of fourteen studies reviewed by Dika and Singh that examined the relationship between social capital and educational achievement, the majority found a positive association between different scores on both counts (Dika and Singh 2002: 41–3). Most of these studies considered achievement in relation to parental social capital; only one found an inverse relationship between achievement and two social capital indicators (parent–school involvement and parental monitoring of progress), while all the remainder were positive. While fewer studies were concerned with students' own connections, these too found positive associations with achievement. However, Dika and Singh point out that much remains unclear about the interplay of various aspects of social capital with academic achievement, and they call for further research into the way that different factors are in turn related to 'access to and mobilisation of social capital' (2002: 43).

Research findings also suggest that social capital may provide a counter-weight to economic and social disadvantage. To date, as already noted, much of the research has looked at the impact of social capital on the education of minority children. Stanton-Salazar and Dornbusch found 'some support' for Coleman's basic hypothesis in their study of social support among Mexican-origin students in Californian high schools, in that those with higher grades and aspirations generally had greater levels of social capital (Stanton-Salazar and Dornbusch 1995: 130). They also found that accessing social capital was more important for bilingual students than for those whose main language was English, suggesting that possibly the Hispanic students were using social capital to compensate for shortfalls in other resources (Stanton-Salazar and Dornbusch 1995: 131–2). As Coleman suggested, then, social capital may offer particularly significant educational resources for those who are otherwise relatively disadvantaged. Unlike Coleman, though, Stanton-Salazar and Dornbusch (1995) found that students' grades were particularly related to the number and range of weak ties, including those that brought people into contact with non-kin and non-Mexican origin members. This emphasis on the role of weak ties in compensating for economic and social disadvantage is something that will be returned to later on in this chapter.

If current research overwhelmingly confirms the significance of social capital, it also poses some serious challenges to Coleman's conceptualisation. The extent to which it is Coleman rather than Bourdieu that has shaped the research agenda in educational studies is remarkable. Yet Coleman viewed social capital as centred primarily on the family, emphasising its role in the young person's cognitive development as well as the degree of social control that it enabled. Coleman argued that geographical mobility tended to disrupt the family's social capital, with damaging consequences for children's education. However, it has been widely discovered that immigrant youth typically do better than expected in school, after allowing for their parents' economic and social circumstances (Stanton-Salazar and Dornbusch 1995; Lauglo 2000). A detailed study of enrolees at four Toronto secondary schools showed that while family moves could reduce high school completion rates for some young people, the loss of community resources was often mitigated by higher levels of direct parental support (Hagan *et al.* 1996: 381). In a survey of young people in Oslo, Lauglo found that youth from developing countries had more constructive attitudes towards school than did all other ethnic groups, while ethnic Norwegians showed such traits least often, and these differences in outlook tended to be mirrored in variations in performance (Lauglo 2000: 149–51). Nor were these patterns found to be related to occupational class or levels of cultural capital, however. As Lauglo points out, then, these patterns are to some extent at odds with aspects of both Coleman's and Bourdieu's theories (Lauglo 2000: 154).

Researchers have also shed critical light on Coleman's rather conservative view of mothering (Morrow 1999). Among other things, Coleman believed that maternal employment was likely to reduce the benefits to children of the family's social capital. He therefore feared that rising employment levels among women were likely to produce long-term damage to the stocks of social capital. Yet an attempt to subject this belief to empirical investigation, using data from the National Longitudinal Survey of Youth, found 'minimally negative effects of early maternal employment on child outcomes'. Basing their findings on test data for young children and patterns of parental employment, the authors confirmed that family generally exercised a significant influence on both verbal facility and behavioural patterns; maternal employment had a negative influence on verbal reasoning alone, and then only where the mother's job was low in skills content; the same study also showed that paternal underemployment could have negative consequences on behavioural problems (Parcel and Menaghan 1994).

Coleman's work can also be criticised for focusing largely on one type of educational institution. Although he was very interested in adolescents' relationships, for example, his investigations of social capital and education were limited to the school stages. He paid little attention to later stages of the formal education system, and none whatever to learning in informal settings such as the workplace. Bourdieu has considered the role of the *grandes écoles* in reproducing privilege among the elites in France, but his major work on the French higher education system is concerned with the deployment of social capital by academics intent on improving their relative position within the scholarly hierarchy rather than with the impact of social capital on students' positions (Bourdieu 1988).

Yet there is no reason to suppose that people cease to enjoy educational advantages arising from their social relationships once they leave school. On the contrary. A much-respected French study of adult learning in a mining community near Lille in the late 1970s showed that while levels of involvement in traditional societies and festivals were similar among participants and non-participants in education, the level of participation in education was much higher among people who were engaged in other, more modern areas of social life which brought them into contact with 'local notables' (Hedoux 1982: 264). This finding contrasts with the results of a more recent study of lifelong learning in Northern Ireland, which shows that while a high level of social capital can reinforce the value placed on school attainment among young people, it can also provide a substitute for organised learning among adults, who may choose to acquire new skills and information informally from neighbours and kin rather than through a more structured course of education or training (Field and Spence 2000; McClenaghan 2000). A similar pattern is found among small firms in Britain, who appear to place a high emphasis on 'learning by doing', mentored more or less formally by role-model figures such as parents, older siblings, friends and trusted older workers, and tend to avoid participation in formal training courses where the outcomes are hard to predict and justify (Hendry et al. 1991: 20–2; Matlay 1997).

There has also been some work on the influence of education on social capital. Partly this is a simple product of proximity. School friends grow up together, and some individuals from each cohort stay in touch over time. But there have been relatively few studies of friendship networks among pupils and students. One survey of social contact patterns among three groups of young Scots – university students, further education students, full-time workers and unemployed people – showed the 'massive advantage of those in full time education as compared with the unemployed' (Emler and McNamara 1996). University students in particular (especially those living away from home) had access to the widest networks and the most frequent contacts, which can be seen as the basis for the weak ties that would secure their future careers. The full-time workers had fewer contacts than the full-time students, but had wider circles of friends than the unemployed (Emler and McNamara 1996: 127). The connection between elite education pathways and membership of networks (neatly summarised in the 'old school tie' metaphor) is well known. It has, though, rarely been conceptualised in terms of social capital.

In broad terms, then, there is an emerging body of research which confirms the impact of social capital on human capital. In general, the research suggests that the influence of social capital is a benign one, in that it is associated with higher levels of performance, and these appear to hold particularly true for young people from disadvantaged backgrounds. In Lauglo's words, social capital can 'trump' the disadvantages of social class and weak cultural capital (Lauglo 2000). As yet, though, it is not clear whether this pattern is a general one which holds good for all forms of disadvantage, or whether it is very dependent upon specific contexts. There is less evidence respecting education after school, but what there is calls into question this simple model of a one-way influence that is largely benign. In some other respects, the evidence on education and social capital also appears to point to the complexity of the relationships which might matter, suggesting that Coleman's model of the family is not sufficiently hearty to carry the conceptual weight that he placed upon it. Despite these qualifications and omissions, the connection between human capital and social capital has rightly been described as 'one of the most robust empirical regularities in the social capital literature' (Glaeser *et al.* 2002: 455). Even if we do not yet fully understand this pattern, we can conclude with some confidence that there is a close relationship between people's social networks and their educational performance.

CONNECTIONS IN THE ECONOMY

There is an abundant and well-established literature on the role of social networks in economic behaviour. It has long been known that personal contacts furnish job seekers with a highly effective way of finding new positions and gaining promotion, while since the 1990s dense networks of firms, researchers and policy-makers have been often seen as decisive factors in enabling innovation and improving competitive performance. More recently, Putnam among others has made the even grander claim that economic performance as a whole is better in well-connected societies than in poorly connected ones (Putnam 1993b, 2000). This section starts by examining studies of social capital in the labour market, then moves on to consider its influence on company performance, before concluding with a brief review of the evidence for Putnam's ambitious claims for a generally positive relationship at the macro-economic level. First, though, it may be helpful to say a few words about the related concept of human capital, which is often mentioned in the same breath as social capital.

Economics is no stranger to the idea that there can be different types of capital. Most important for the purposes of this analysis, economists have been interested in the concept of human capital since the early 1960s. Initially, the concept was introduced as a way of drawing attention to the contribution of labour to company performance; Schultz proposed that the potential value of labour's contribution could rise, given appropriate investment, for example in the form of skills training (Schultz 1961). This broadly humanistic emphasis rapidly gave way to a more technically sophisticated approach to modelling the relationship between investment in human capital, on the one hand, and the rate of return to that investment, on the other. In the hands of the eminent neo-classical economist Gary Becker (1964), human capital thinking was turned into a tool for judging the effectiveness of different types of investment (such as job-specific training and general education), and calculating the distribution of returns as between, say, the employer, the government and the individual them-selves. Becker worked at the University of Chicago, as did Coleman, with whom he worked on the application of rational choice theory during the early 1980s. While Becker certainly embraced the notion of social capital, he placed it in an even more individualistic framework than Coleman, and made little impact on the wider debate over the concept (Fine and Green 2000: 82). However, his notion of human capital has provided an important backdrop to the reception of the concept of social capital, and may have helped prepare the ground for its adoption by such leading mainstream bodies as the World Bank.

Early work on the job search behaviour of migrants and young workers during the 1970s had limited impact on the wider debate over human capital among economists, most of whom tended to see qualifications and schooling as the source of employability. Yet is hardly surprising that family, supported by other kinship-based connections, has played an important role in job search. For most of the industrial era, family connections continued to provide the main basis for recruitment. Until the late 1980s, for instance, it was necessary in Britain for parents – usually the father – to sign the indenture that marked the start of apprenticeship training; as Lorna Unwin points out, this marked a strong two-way commitment between parents and workplace, with clear expectations on either side (Unwin 1996). What is significant is the extent to which family and friendship networks have continued to dominate job search into the post-industrial age, and in very different types of society. Half of young people in Spain in a 1996 survey had entered work thanks to family and friends (Viscarnt 1998: 244). In a study of young people who had grown up in the German Democratic Republic, Volker and Flap found that the individual's education played a more important role than the father's resources in finding work; never-theless, nearly half of their sample had found work through informal channels, and in these cases it was often important to possess strong ties with highly prestigious contacts (Volker and Flap 1999).

This pattern appears to hold good for adult workers as well as school leavers. In a study of job search among unemployed Swedes, Thomas Korpi found that the size of an individual's personal network had a considerable positive impact on the likelihood of finding work. He estimated that the value of each additional contact was as great or greater than that of utilising other search channels, including the formal employment agency (Korpi 2001: 166). In China, laid-off workers who found another job did so overwhelmingly by using their social capital, which typically consisted of kin and close neighbours (Zhao 2002: 563–4). A Canadian study of long-term welfare recipients during the mid-1990s showed that the influence of social capital on the likelihood of welfare exit was greater than that of any other factor, including human capital and demographic characteristics (Lévesque and White 2001). In Spain, it was found that unemployed people relied overwhelmingly on the Instituto Nacional de Empleo; lacking effective contacts, they were forced to turn to a public agency whose results were minimal, and they therefore remained unemployed (Viscarnt 1998: 245). Finally, Aguilera (2002) has found that social capital – as measured through friendship networks – was positively associated with labour force participation, suggesting that those who are well connected are not only likely to find work when they search, but are more likely to be active in the labour market in the first place.

Most of these accounts have focused on the supply side – that is, the job seekers and their networks. Relatively few empirical studies have explored the demand side of the labour market; the perspective from the employer's side often tends to be overlooked or taken for granted. However, one detailed analysis of hiring patterns in an American call centre has showed that reliance on networks and contacts can produce significant economic returns (Fernandez *et al.* 2000). This particular company had chosen to pay existing employees who referred acquaintances; the going rate at the time of the study was $10 for each referral who was interviewed, rising to $250 for each referral who was hired and remained for at least 30 days. The study found that the firm made savings at several stages of the hiring process: fewer referrals were rejected at application stage; fewer fell out on interview; and fewer turned down an offer. The total difference between referrals and non-referrals came to $416.43 per recruit, a return of 67 per cent on the initial investment of $250 (Fernandez *et al.* 2000: 1347–8). But the differences persisted after the new workers had entered the company, as people recruited through referral were less likely to leave and more likely themselves to become sources of new referrals in the future.

Granovetter's pioneering work famously emphasised the value of what he called 'weak ties', which gave job seekers access to a wider range of information about a more diverse set of opportunities (Granovetter 1973). However, this clearly has to be offset against the greater effort which close connections will make to find the person a job. Over half of Korpi's sample approached no friends and relatives while unemployed; those who did almost always approached strong connections only (Korpi 2001: 164). He concluded that there was no clear evidence of any difference in terms of outcome between those who used strong and weak ties (Korpi 2001: 167). Importantly, then, bonding social capital appears to be as effective as bridging social capital (see below, pages 65–6) in helping both young entrants to the labour market and unemployed adults to find work.

While the debate about personal connections and the labour market is a mature one, the idea that social capital influences competitiveness is a more recent one. Economic policy and research were both stimulated during the 1980s, partly in response to the emergence of dynamic industrial companies and regions in Japan; it was often suggested that one cause of Japanese industrial success was the importance of outsourcing, underpinned by well-coordinated supply chains. As a result, supply chains and regional networks came to be seen as a new and effective way of coordinating firms and other business partners (Karnøe 1999). As with labour market studies, though, this body of work has only recently started to use the concept of social capital (Maskell 2000), partly under the stimulus of repeated assertions from Putnam (1993a; 1993b; 2000: 319–25) and Francis Fukuyama (1995) concerning the positive economic consequences of social capital.

Networks have long been seen as important to business success. Particularly during the start-up stage, it is widely accepted that networks function as an important information resource, which can be critical in identifying and exploiting business opportunities (Hendry et al. 1991: 16; Mulholland 1997: 703–6). They can also help provide access to finance (Bates 1994: 674). Social capital has also been regarded as an asset in respect of markets and labour; even when recruited through intermediaries, both customers and workers are said to show greater loyalty and commitment than might be the case among total strangers (Bates 1994: 674–7; Jones et al. 1993). Networks are also thought to contribute towards a consistent and stable management style, which can in turn be vital in enabling firms to withstand external shocks, particularly in boom–bust sectors like construction (Hendry et al. 1991: 17). In her study of social capital among managers, Erika Hayes James has found that tie strength is particularly important as a source of psychosocial support, which can be drawn on when the going gets tough (James 2000: 503). Of course, social capital alone is not enough. Successful family businesses in Britain, according to one study, are usually led by well-educated individuals who already have good access to both social *and* financial capital (Mulholland 1997: 707). All the same, the idea that social capital can contribute positively to organisational performance seems to be widely accepted, and well founded in the evidence.

In recent years, there has been considerable interest in the role of networks and clusters in promoting business innovation and knowledge exchange (Porter 2000; Le Bas *et al*. 1998). Knowledge is a notoriously fragile commodity, in that sellers have little protection from unscrupulous behaviour by buyers, other than the high cost option of legal action; knowledge therefore tends to be exchanged far less freely than is optimal for business performance. Trust-based relations between entrepreneurs may help compensate against these risks, and can reduce a variety of transaction costs (most obviously the legal costs of patent protection, but also the search costs of identifying relevant techniques and technologies, as well as those of converting them into usable forms). The depth and range of such trust-based relations have been held to explain the otherwise unexpected success of the small Nordic economies, which appear to combine high labour costs with a capacity to compete in globalised markets (Maskell *et al*. 1998). In the case of the Danish furniture industry, which is typically a highly competitive sector of small firms that are low on technological innovation and high on labour costs, it has been suggested that 'it is perhaps impossible to overstate the importance' of 'the social community of managers', particularly in the solution of day-to-day problems (Henriksen 1999: 256). Similar findings exist for other contexts. A statistical analysis of correlation between social capital and a range of other factors among Tanzanian farmers suggested that it produced greater prosperity by promoting the diffusion of innovation, overcoming information deficits in markets, and providing informal insurance in the event of unforeseen difficulty, all of which in turn led to changes in farming practices (Narayan and Pritchett 1999). And in the international hotel industry in Sydney, it has been estimated that each friendship between managers of competing hotels in Sydney makes a contribution to annual revenue of some Aus$268,000 (Ingram and Roberts 2000: 417).

Innovation exchange, as well as more established inter-firm activity such as the trading of goods and services, appears to be promoted by the existence of stable networks of people who trust one another. Cooperation, particularly between competitors, is facilitated by the norms of trust that are embedded in inter- and intra-firm networks. These norms are valuable firstly in that they allow businesses to trade with one another without relying solely on formal mechanisms and procedures, such as legally binding contracts or lawsuits, which are both slow and costly. This role of social capital in reducing transaction costs is widely recognised in the social capital literature (Putnam 2000: 288; Fukuyama 1995: Ch. 5). But high-trust networks often go beyond the basics of conducting business with a minimum of formality. As we have seen, it can also extend to the exchange of sensitive information and ideas with competitors. Moreover, much of the most relevant knowledge seems to be essentially applied in nature: it concerns not only the abstract science ('know-what') but also its application in embedded settings ('know-how') by people who develop substantial but often tacit expertise ('know-who') (Maskell 2000). This dual process represents a much higher level of coordination than is often recognised.

This insight directly contradicts much contemporary management thinking about labour and innovation, resting as it does on the belief that a high level of turnover brings in fresh youthful minds who will embrace novelty and adapt to change. Yet this strategy, by disrupting existing networks, can have exactly the opposite effect on performance. One study of high-tech firms in Silicon Valley found a 'significant negative effect of turnover on revenue growth' (Baron *et al.* 2001: 1006). Rather than leading to innovation and flexibility, turnover was removing firm-specific knowledge and disrupting the 'organisational blueprint' which had been preserved by old-guard workers (Baron *et al.* 2001: 1002).

Some firms, by contrast, deliberately exploit these positive aspects of social capital. For example, a study of financial advisers in French banks noted that personnel departments encouraged greater internal flexibility partly in order to enable financial advisers to accumulate and optimise their social capital, which in turn helped them to increase their business (Ferrary 2002). One British study suggested that an increasing proportion of more successful ethnic minority business heads had joined predominantly white clubs as part of a strategy designed to help build reliable networks (Mulholland 1997: 706). Of course, this is not as simple as it might sound. The authors of the Sydney hotel study concluded that the most trusting relationships are those that are multi-dimensional, resting on mutual affection as well as instrumental reciprocity (Ingram and Roberts 2000). In order to exploit fully the potential benefits of their networks, then, business people actually have to do more than move around the company or join the right clubs. They actually need to enjoy one another's company.

Finally, what of Putnam's claim (2000: 319) that 'where trust and social networks flourish, individuals, firms, neighborhoods and even nations prosper'? At the macro-level, the evidence appears to be suggestive rather than conclusive. Putnam concluded from his earlier study of Italian democracy that there was a long-term association between civic engagement and prosperity, which he attributed to the development of habits of cooperation and norms of trust. Knack and Keefer (1997) used World Values Survey data to show that general interpersonal trust is positively associated with economic growth, even when controlling for other factors. However, their study found no correlation between growth rate and membership in associations. Paul Whiteley has compared rates of economic growth with a broad range of social capital indicators based on the World Values Survey for thirty-four countries, finding that there is at least a strong an association as there is between human capital and rate of growth (Whiteley 2000). This study offers few clues as to why this association should be so strong, but it is supported by the more detailed work of Narayan and Pritchett, who estimate, in their study of rural Tanzania, that variations in social capital at the level of the village had greater influence on income levels than equivalent changes in either human capital or physical assets (Narayan and Pritchitt 1999: 274).

At the macro-level, claims of a clear link between social capital and economic growth are as yet unproven. Part of the problem, as the OECD has pointed out, lies in the quality of the evidence at this level of analysis:

> As in the case of human capital, the evidence is affected by the quality and breadth of proxy measures, the complexity of inter-relationships between different conditioning factors, and the difficulty in comparing countries with widely differing cultural, institutional and historical traditions.
>
> (OECD 2001b: 61)

Yet if we lack robust evidence to demonstrate that social capital is generally related to growth rates, there is enough to suggest that there may be specific conditions under which it is an important part of the explanation. The possibility of a relationship should, then, certainly not be ignored.

Economics as a discipline frequently tends to treat decision-making as an individual process, and traditionally economists have not paid much attention to the ways in which individual behaviour and choices are embedded in a wider social context. Concepts like networks and trust are too imprecise to be imported into a neat formula, and, anyway, their meaning for people often depends on their context, making them very difficult for mainstream economists to tackle. As Sanjaya Lall points out, neo-classical economic theory rests on a paradigm of perfect competition, and 'shies away from dealing with widespread and diffuse externalities and fuzzy learning phenomena' (Lall 2000: 14). From the perspective of other social sciences, economics appears to be 'infamous for its methodological individualism, by which society is to be understood merely by aggregating the behaviour of its constituent quasi-autonomous individuals' (Fine and Green 2000: 80). Many economists have, though, long known that embeddness counts. While the concept of social capital is a relative newcomer to these discussions, it has been embraced by the World Bank and the OECD as well as by a number of academic economists, and this has helped to restate the importance of social relations for mainstream economics.

BENEFITS FOR HEALTH AND WELL-BEING

The idea that social cohesion and health are related is at least century old. In the late nineteenth century, Durkheim showed that suicide rates were higher in populations with low levels of social integration, and lower in closely knit communities. Evidence of a more general association between health levels and social ties has been well established since the late 1970s, showing that people with strong social networks had mortality rates half or a third of those with weak social ties (Whitehead and Diderichsen 2001). Putnam (2000) has been able to draw on a large number of subsequent studies – which have tried to control for other characteristics, such as age, income and even patterns of behaviour such as smoking, drinking and exercise – that generally confirm the importance of this link. For example, in an influential study of international data on mortality and social inequality, Richard Wilkinson showed that social cohesion appeared to serve as a powerful independent variable, along of course with other reasonably well-established factors such as material deprivation (Wilkinson 1996). He also found some evidence that social inequality tends to reduce social stability and undermines social networks, leading to higher levels of anxiety, stress and ill health. Similar comparative research in the USA by Kawachi and his colleagues, who isolated social capital more clearly than Wilkinson, confirmed the broad association that he had identified between health and social cohesion (Kawachi *et al.* 1997a). Putnam, moreover, was also able to show a very clear positive correlation at state level between a range of health indicators and his Social Capital Index, along with a strong negative association between the SCI and mortality rates (Putnam 2000: 328–31).

Further evidence for this link continues to accumulate. A Finnish comparison between the health of the Swedish-speaking minority with the rest of the population suggested that the lower mortality rates and longer lives of the minority – whose diet and lifestyles do not differ – were associated with 'inequalities in social integration' (Hyppä and Mäki 2001). A comparative study of local communities in the old South Yorkshire coalfield showed that higher levels of reciprocity are closely associated with higher health scores (Green *et al.* 2000: 29). An analysis of data from a range of American government and health service surveys produced findings that were consistent with the belief that higher levels of social capital can enable better access to health care (Hendryx *et al.* 2002). It has even been suggested on the basis of a large-scale Swedish study that an extensive social network helps protect against dementia (OECD 2001b: 53). The evidence that people with more social capital are likely to live longer, and suffer from fewer health disorders, is reasonably conclusive.

To date, though, the precise reasons for these associations is far from clear (Macinko and Starfield 2001). Putnam has speculated that there might be four reasons for the link between social capital and health. First, he points out that social networks can furnish tangible material assistance, which in turn reduces stress; second, they can reinforce healthy norms; third, they can lobby more effectively for medical services; and finally, interaction may actually help stimulate the body's immune system (Putnam 2000: 327). Unsurprisingly, then, Putnam is alarmed at the possible consequences of an apparent decline in social capital in the USA.

Recent research sheds some light on the nature of the connection. First, it seems that Putnam is right to anticipate that the well-connected are better at lobbying for medical services. However, this appears also to be associated with better communications and accountability mechanisms, so that people in well-connected communities are well placed to influence local health services, are better informed about them, and are also more likely to be able to access them (Hendryx *et al.* 2002).

Health is not just a matter of accessing services, but also of adopting a lifestyle that promotes well-being and helps avoid risks such as obesity. If people are going to change their behaviour and adopt a healthier lifestyle, they are more likely to do so if they learn the new patterns from people they trust, and believe that the changes may actually make a difference. It has been suggested in a study of child health that people's social capital is associated with their sense of self-worth and self-efficacy, and their belief in their capacity to take action over their lives. The health effects are therefore likely to be positive ones (Morrow 1999: 745). Both trust and self-confidence are likely to be facilitated by a rich, stable and dense network of relationships (Campbell 2000: 186).

Of course, as in other areas, social capital alone is not enough. Well-networked communities often tend to be more prosperous (see below), and levels of income tend to have an impact on levels of health. An overview of health survey research in England suggests that socio-economic situation and income are the strongest predictors of health levels, rather than social capital; while social capital was found to be an important variable, it is often combined with other factors (Cooper *et al*. 1999). A more small-scale and intensive study of health and social capital in two neighbourhoods in Luton, England, also questioned whether the resources available in these communities were in fact capable of functioning as Putnam claims (Campbell *et al*. 1999). Most people's networks in Luton were relatively restricted and small-scale, and they were also comparatively informal, with little capacity for generating generalised trust; the authors suggest that some types of network are better than others at promoting healthy behaviour, and that there may be important inequalities of access – for example, associated with income and ethnicity – to these networks. This would lead to the hypothesis that in respect of health, it is highly likely that vertical ties between different groups up and down the social ladder are a decisive factor (Whitehead and Diderichsen 2001). Horizontal ties – that is, those which create bonds between individuals in the same community or social group – seem to have few if any beneficial effects on health. If this is correct, it may help explain Wilkinson's (1996) finding that, over time, countries with more equal income distributions also have higher life expectancies.

Studies of health and social capital have also thrown up a rather important methodological question. Among others, Whitehead and Diderichsen have asked how far we can generalise individual findings to cover a whole population. It has long been known, for example, that at individual level there is a close association between health and social relationships; people with strong social networks have markedly lower mortality rates, and lack of supportive relationships is associated with coronary disease (Whitehead and Diderichsen 2001). Yet it is not clear whether this should allow scholars to extrapolate from individual differences of this kind to whole populations, for example at the national level. Some health researchers, moreover, have warned against the elision of psychological and social indicators (Whitehead and Diderichsen 2001). Whitehead and Diderichsen claim that psychological perceptions of trust and control should be distinguished carefully from such features of the social environment as government policies or housing segregation. These methodological questions are important ones, and deserve closer attention. Yet the general pattern of the evidence at present does suggest a broadly positive relationship between social capital and health.

CRIME AND DEVIANCY

Social dislocation has long been fingered as a cause of crime. The English journalist Henry Mayhew reported in the middle of the nineteenth century on what he thought was the impact of urbanisation and the growth of slum life upon criminality. Since Durkheim, social scientists have investigated the links between social control and levels of crime. Jane Jacobs, who is often credited with introducing the concept of social capital into contemporary sociology, developed the concept partly to explain why some cities are safer places than others (Jacobs 1961). Coleman's early work explored what he saw as the negative influence of peer opinion on adolescents, as already noted. Some forty years on, the role of social influences on youth delinquency is now extremely well known (Haynie 2001). Putnam produced a strong negative association at state level between violent crime and the Social Capital Index, claiming that higher 'levels of social capital, all else being equal, translate into lower levels of crime' (Putnam 2000: 308).

As in the other areas reviewed above, there is no shortage of research showing that the association between social capital and crime is generally benign. Structural equation modelling has been used to explore the relationship between homicide and a number of other factors, including social capital (using data for trust and civic engagement from the General Social Survey), for ninety-nine areas across the USA (Rosenfeld *et al*. 2001). The authors of this study reported that while economic deprivation, divorce rate and Southern location were also serious factors, social capital exercised 'a significant effect on homicide rates, net of the other predictors', while unemployment rate and age composition of the population had no effect (Rosenfield *et al*. 2001: 294). According to the authors, crime was a product of weak informal social controls and low capacity to mobilise such formal external resources as the law enforcement agencies (Rosenfeld *et al.* 2001: 286–7).

As in many other areas, though, it is by no means clear from Putnam's account as to why this equation should hold good, other than the general tendency of delinquent peers to influence other young people into crime, and of positive role models and support networks to lead kids away from crime (Putnam 2000: 310–13). Nevertheless, there are some clear indicators in more recent and detailed work of the nature of the link between social capital and the tendency to abide by the law. Much recent research is North American, and points to the deterrent role of strong networks. Criminality appears generally to thrive in neighbourhoods where most people do not know one another all that well, where supervision of teenage peer groups is minimal, and where civic engagement (including engagement with the law enforcement system) is low (OECD 2001b: 54). Even in such a fluid and dynamic society as contemporary Chicago, the greater the cohesion and shared expectations of the wider community, the lower the rates of crime and disorder (Sampson and Raudenbush 1999). However, some researchers suggest that social capital might kick in at an earlier stage, giving people the confidence and respect to intervene before behaviour gets out of hand, for example by discouraging teenagers from forming threatening groups on the street, or taking drugs (Halpern 2001). Strong networks can also provide a context where young people acquire a sense of status and self-esteem that promotes their integration into the wider community, with a particularly marked impact in reducing the prospect of violent crime (Kawachi *et al.* 1997b). And, as ever, social capital is never the only influence at work. Much criminal behaviour, for example, is closely associated with material inequality (it is worth stating that it is inequality that appears to prompt crime, rather than poverty as such). Drawing on data for eighteen countries from the International Crime Victim Survey, Halpern has found that well over half of the variation in reported crime rates could be explained by cross-country variations in economic inequality, social trust, and what he defines as 'self-interested' values (Halpern 2001).

Social capital can, then, be seen as one factor among others that helps to influence the amount of criminal activity in a community. It also seems to play a part in determining whether or not particular individuals turn to criminal behaviour. Nor is this simply a matter of how the community and its members behave; social capital can also shape the behaviour of law enforcement agencies. Social capital may also have a bearing on people's respect for law enforcement agencies, not least because the police and other institutions are likely to function more effectively where networks are strong and levels of normative integration are high. And of course, this is a self-reinforcing pattern. Communities with low levels of crime, and high regard for and from the police, will be communities which find it easy to develop and maintain effective social ties. By contrast, a sudden and sharp breakdown in social capital – as occurred in many of Britain's coalmining communities after the national strike and pit closures of the 1980s – is invariably accompanied by an intractable rise in alienation and anti-social behaviour, particularly among young males.

REFINING THE CONCEPT: RECIPROCITY AND TRUST

A growing literature has emerged which largely agrees on the broad impact of social capital upon people's well-being. Being connected is in itself a resource, in so far as socialising with others is a rewarding experience in its own right, but people are also able to make use of their connections to obtain other benefits. As this brief review of recent research evidence shows, there appear to be clear and often strong positive links between social capital and educational attainment, economic success, health and freedom from crime. No one would claim that social capital alone can explain all the variations in these areas, but it is now clear that neither should anyone ignore its significance among other factors. Yet social capital is a relatively young concept, and much more needs to be known about the variety of ways in which social ties work to engender such significant effects. A number of writers have suggested that in order for people to cooperate to achieve their goals, they have not only to have some previous knowledge of one another (which may be direct or indirect), they also need to trust one another, and expect that if they cooperate then they will not be exploited or defrauded, but can at some time or other expect to benefit similarly in return.

Coleman and Putnam were at one in defining trust as one key component of social capital. As early as the 1980s, for example, Coleman himself was writing on the importance of trust in economic life, and accusing economists of ignoring the qualitative change that occurs in the transition from the micro-level of the individual to the macro-level of a system composed of individuals (Swedberg 1996: 316–17). While Bourdieu does not specifically mention trust, it is clearly implicit in his argument of social reproduction that people who intermarry or club together in order to expand their useful connections must do so on some basis of trust. Francis

Fukuyama has gone furthest, defining trust itself as a basic feature of social capital: 'Social capital is a capability that arises from the prevalence of trust in a society or in certain parts of it' (Fukuyama 1995: 26). The political scientist Eric Uslaner has followed Fukuyama in arguing that social capital reflects 'primarily a system of values, especially social trust' (Uslaner 1999: 122). Fukuyama himself, though, has even claimed that trust is the very basis of social order: 'Communities depend on mutual trust and will not arise spontaneously without it' (Fukuyama 1995: 25).

The role of trust has itself been widely discussed across the social sciences, to the point where the literature has become quite dense and specialised. This section will only consider this issue in so far as it is relevant to our discussion of social capital, rather than covering its wider treatment in sociological and economic debate (however, see Glaeser *et al*. 2000; Luhmann 1988; Misztal 1996; Sztompka 1999). The importance of trust can be seen across a variety of situations where we engage with others: sleeping with someone, using a credit card, getting married, taking a plane, picking a meal for one's children, wondering whether to report a crime, deciding how to vote, and choosing between different ways of saving the environment (or not). Trust and trustworthiness have often been compared to a lubricant, oiling the wheels of a variety of social and economic transactions which might otherwise prove extremely costly, bureaucratic and time-consuming. This is highly relevant to the concept of social capital, which emphasises the way in which networks give access to resources.

Self-evidently, a high-trust network will function more smoothly and easily than is the case for a low-trust one. Anyone who has experienced betrayal by an intimate partner will know how difficult it is for two people to cooperate when their behaviour lacks a basis in trust. But trust is not only based on face-to-face relations between two or more people. It can be an attribute of institutions and groups as well as individuals, and is often based on reputation which is mediated through third parties (Dasgupta 2000: 333). Much of the literature around trust distinguishes between particularised trust, which is limited to an individual's own observations and experience over time of a particular actor's trustworthiness, and generalised trust, which may be extended to all individuals and institutions resembling those of whom one has direct experience. Beyond this, Luhmann has further distinguished a general propensity to trust in trust itself (Luhmann 1988). From the perspective of a discussion of social capital, it is clear that these different dimensions of trust might represent varied ways of accessing resources.

Trust plays a vital role in gaining access to some benefits of social networks. For example, trust may be particularly important in respect of access to assets such as knowledge, which are relatively intangible and sometimes tacit. We have already seen one vivid example in the case of the call centre which chooses to recruit new staff through recommendations from existing employees, rather than spending time and money on advertising and notifying the job centre. Generally, it is known in economics that when knowledge is passed on, the seller finds it difficult to obtain a continuing income (or rent). This means that information-flows between firms are often imperfect, because the people who already hold a particular piece of knowledge are better off keeping it to themselves than selling it on. The law of intellectual copyright is one attempt to solve this problem, but it involves very considerable transaction costs. From this perspective, legal procedures and bureaucratic hierarchies mainly exist because trust is not, and never can be, ubiquitous. Trust-based relations offer a low cost alternative to lawyers' fees, and help reduce the risk and uncertainty involved in acquiring knowledge which can promote innovation and thereby enhance competition (Maskell *et al.* 1998: 43–4). Particularly among economists, then, there is a good case for considering trust to be an important issue in the debate over social capital.

Yet a number of commentators doubt whether trust is to be treated as an integral component of social capital or as one of its outcomes. First, it should be noted that trust itself is a complex and varied phenomenon, and its integration into the concept of social capital along with other factors (networks and norms) makes the concept an extremely complicated one. Second, trust is not a necessary consequence of shared norms and strong networks, and may therefore be best treated as a separate variable. Many relationships can operate perfectly well with a minimum of trust, including many of those which rest on habit or institutional sanction rather than on reflexive choice. Third, as Rose notes, drawing an analytical distinction between trust and social capital makes it possible to construct a cause-and-effect model of the relationship between the two (Rose 1999: 151). And indeed, from a sociological perspective Woolcock argues that trust may best be seen as a consequence of social capital over time (Woolcock 2001: 13). Fourth, it is far from clear that trust in itself is desirable. Fukuyama in particular offers a highly simplified account, which largely accords to the self-image of corporate America (Schuller *et al.* 2000: 17). Mistrust in management may be a prudent stance by workers who fear lay-offs and wage cuts; mistrust of government may be a healthy aspect of modern democracy; mistrust is a sensible attitude towards a philandering lover. Trust is certainly related closely to social capital, conceptually and empirically, and it will emerge time and again in the rest of this book as one of the most important resources to arise from membership in social networks. Yet it is almost certainly best treated as an independent factor, which is generally a consequence rather than an integral component of social capital.

TOWARDS A DIFFERENTIATED CONCEPTION

This discussion of trust has revealed further complexities in the concept of social capital. Initial uses of the term have inevitably been rather perfunctory, and even sloganistic in nature. In attempting to draw attention to a rather neglected aspect of human behaviour and institutions, some writers have tended to paint a somewhat simplistic picture of the social ties that they were describing. Coleman's usage, as already shown, has tended almost entirely to represent close and direct ('primordial') interpersonal ties; Putnam's has tended to paint warm images of community; Bourdieu has drawn a particularised and instrumental picture of connections as a buttress of privilege. So far this chapter has made little attempt to unpack the complexities of social capital. Rather, the main focus has been on a review of the evidence for social capital's importance. Nevertheless, this evidence has itself pointed to the need for a more differentiated concept which is capable of tying together the micro-, meso- and macro-levels of social analysis.

Of the founding authors, the one who has gone furthest in embracing a differentiated approach to social capital is Putnam. In his more recent work, Putnam has followed Michael Woolcock and others in distinguishing between 'bonding' and 'bridging' forms of social capital (Putnam 2000: 22–4; Woolcock 1998). For Putnam, bonding (or 'exclusive') social capital is based around family, close friends and other near kin; it is inward-looking and binds people from a similar sociological niche; it tends to 'reinforce exclusive identities and homogenous groups'. By contrast, bridging (or 'inclusive') social capital links people to more distant acquaintances who move in different circles from their own; it tends to generate broader identities and wider reciprocity rather than reinforcing a narrow grouping. Putnam believes that while bonding social capital is good for 'getting by', bridging social capital is crucial for 'getting ahead'. Woolcock has developed this binary distinction, which he sees as horizontal, so as to incorporate a third, vertical dimension of 'linking' social capital that consists of relationships up and down the social and economic scale (Woolcock 2001: 13). The importance of linking social capital is that it allows people to leverage resources, ideas and information from contacts outside their own social milieu. This idea has particular practical importance for community development policies and other anti-poverty strategies (see below, Chapter 5).

The basic distinction between bridging and bonding social capital has been widely accepted. Some have resorted to a rather different terminology from that advocated by Putnam and Woolcock. Nan Lin, for example, distinguishes between 'strong ties' and 'weak ties' (Lin 2001: Ch. 5). Lin's terminology follows that of Mark Granovetter, whose early studies of job search among young people suggested that while strong ties were a good source of jobs in firms and occupations where family and close friends were already represented, weak ties were a relatively effective way of finding jobs in new fields (Granovetter 1973). Lin defines strong ties as those which follow the principle of 'homophily', binding people with others similar to themselves; weak ties bring together people from different social and cultural backgrounds. Lin also contrasts the kinds of resources and purposes which different types of social capital can deliver. While strong ties bring together individuals and groups with rather similar resources, in order to purse normative and identity-based goals (what Lin defines as 'expressive' purposes), weak ties may be better at serving instrumental goals as they can provide access to new types of resources but rely less on strongly shared values. Lin develops these insights to theorise a model of social capital that incorporates the distinction between strong and weak ties (or bridging and bonding social capital), the purposes of mutual cooperation (expressive and instrumental), actors' structural social positions, and membership of networks that provide access to positions (Lin 2001: 75–6).

Some writers have attempted to operationalise these distinctions and see whether they have the explanatory force attributed to them. In general, it seems that homogeneity and heterogeneity appear to be an important factor in determining how social capital functions. To take one example, a study of social capital among women and male entrepreneurs found that the women generally had more homogeneous networks than the men, and in particular were more likely to rely on kin as network members (Renzulli et al. 2000). Apparently, these distinctive network characteristics formed an independent variable which could help explain the relative performance of male and female entrepreneurs. In her study of Russia's 'economy of favours', Ledeneva found that the most effective operators had both horizontal and vertical links, and so were able not only both to secure and supply favours, but functioned at the centre of networks. In this system of *blat*, or the systematic use of informal contacts, such people were seen as the *Blatmeisters* (Ledeneva 1998: 124). So understanding the nature and scope of the ties between individuals, communities and/or institutions can be helpful in enabling us to grasp the different ways in which social capital delivers access to a variety of resources.

So far, these distinctions have rested mainly on the question of social ties. What of the values that also constitute an important dimension of social capital? In an ambitious attempt to combine the structural and normative dimension of people's networks, Pamela Paxton has defined social capital as constituted of two different components, each of which may operate independently of the other (Paxton 1999: 94–6). The two components of Paxton's definition are (a) the level of associations between individuals or the objective network structure, on the one hand, and (b) the subjective ties between the same individuals, on the other. To illustrate their independence, she presents a simple table which disaggregates the effects of the two different components (Figure 2.1). Social capital is present, according to Paxton, when both variables are high. When associations are high but the subjective ties are low, actors may need to resort to other (more costly) ways of securing cooperation, such as a legally binding contract. When the subjective ties are high but associations are low, then goodwill may exist but it is likely that intermediaries will be needed in order to overcome the barriers to effective cooperation.

Paxton has also distinguished between the effects of social capital at individual level and its effects at community level. She is certainly not the only author to make this distinction, but she goes on to argue that the concept can be considered at multiple levels, rather than insisting – as do others – that it should be considered either one or the other. Importantly, though, 'social capital *within a single group* need not be positively related to social capital *at the community level*' (Paxton 1999: 96; original emphasis). Indeed, the existence of tight-within-group social capital may work against the existence of strong ties at the level of the wider community. One example might be the close bonds developed within the two main religious traditions in Northern Ireland, which have generally enabled Catholics to cooperate very effectively with fellow Catholics, and Protestants with fellow Protestants, but which preclude social capital between the two groups.

		Associations between individuals	
		High	Low
Subjective ties between individuals	High	A social capital	B
	Low	C	D

Figure 2.1 Paxton's model of social capital

Paxton's model offers one useful way of explaining the weight of different types of linkage. However, it should be used with some caution. In particular, she oversimplifies considerably in suggesting that social capital is present only in Box A, where objective network ties are complemented by strong subjective bonds. Social capital may well be unequally distributed between the four boxes, but can nevertheless be said to exist in each. In particular, social capital is likely to be stronger in B and C than in D. Paxton's model comes close to representing social capital as a zero-sum asset, rather than as a variable which is highly dependent on context and history.

A further distinction needs to be made in respect of the human capital that is required to activate social capital. Even when people are members of a variety of networks, with varying levels of shared values, they still have to learn the skills required in order to benefit from cooperation. The acquisition and development of social competences has not so far been an aspect of social capital that has attracted much attention (though Bourdieu's ideas about cultural capital may offer an important pointer). Inevitably, the skills needed for different types of network are differentially distributed.

Some of the ways in which skills are distributed appear to follow gender lines; for example, Morrow speculates that many of the rules of networking may vary between women and men. Particularly where networks are characterised by affective ties, emotionally valued skills and assets are an important resource, which may be more readily available to women as a result of their '(historical) concentration in the private sphere' (Morrow 1999: 755). Moreover, because these ties are based around neighbourhood and kinship, they are less vulnerable to such economic shocks as unemployment than are men's (Russell 1999: 210). Differential changes in access to networks after unemployment may in turn affect the balance of power within families. I would guess that there are also important social class differences in the way that networking skills are distributed, particularly in a country like Britain, where the association between schooling and social class is so marked; and there are possibly regional/national and ethnic variations as well. Many of the skills required to access the different resources made available through people's networks are tacit ones, which are deeply embedded in the practice of the relationships themselves. This quality may, of course, help explain the great difficulties of transferring one's social capital from one context to another, or of translating it into another type of capital.

Finally, we need to differentiate between the uses that different individuals may make of their social capital. Social capital has a micro-level dimension, situated as it is within the many varied lifeworlds that make up individuals' biographies. One useful example of this is the way that different types of social capital may be important at different times within the individual's life course. Pahl and Spencer, for example, suggest that close ties (bonding social capital) are vital in providing physical and mental support during early childhood and frail old age, while looser ties (bridging social capital) can also provide useful resources when negotiating the risks, changes and uncertainties of adult life (Pahl and Spencer 1997: 102). As a result, 'being able to acquire or access different types of social capital at different times in one's life may therefore be crucial to an individual's quality of life' (Performance and Innovation Unit 2002: 26; see also Warde et al. 1999).

In conclusion, there is a wide range of research into social capital, and considerable interest in its role in explaining differences in people's life chances. Indeed, so wide-ranging have the usages been that some already warn against the 'over-versatility' (Thompson 2002) of an idea that is still relatively young and untested. Yet it is not so new as all that. As the previous chapter showed, the idea that relationships are a resource appeared together with modern social theory, and was elaborated by Marx, Durkheim, Simmel and Weber among others. What, then, can be said to be new about the concept of social capital? In particular, is it simply a fancy way of dressing up aging debates about the nature of community? The answer – and thereby the claim to conceptual distinctiveness – is surely indicated in the use of the notion of *capital*. The parallel with financial capital or physical capital is deliberate, and implies that social capital produces returns that in some way benefit its holders. In its weakest, most general formulation, the claim is simply that social capital is a resource, which can be used by actors to help them achieve their goals. In a more ambitious sense of the term, the notion of capital is to be taken, quite literally, as denoting an embodied productive investment in social relationships, leading to a measurable return which may then benefit those who made the investment (Schuller 2000). In either case, though, it is the existence of positive benefits that allow us to use the language of capital.

Social capital serves to provide these returns by creating the pre-requisites for cooperation and reciprocity. Lin suggests that there are a number of central mechanisms that lead to this outcome, including (a) information, (b) influence through intermediaries, (c) confirmation of trustworthiness, and (d) reinforcement of promises and commitments (Lin 2001: 18–19). However, as Coleman has noted, the value of network membership is not limited to the actors who have invested knowingly in it; much of the investment is not intentionally made as such, but rather is made in order to serve actors' own purposes; and its value is often as much for the broader public good as for those individuals who actually belong to and have invested in the network. Much of this chapter has focussed on the evidence that social capital does indeed produce clear positive returns for network members and the community at large, before going on to explore some of the complexity of networks and norms, and identify the implications for our understanding of social capital. So far, I have focussed on the types of return that are almost invariably welcomed, and can therefore be seen as positive not only for network members but also others in the wider community. Given what we know about conflict and inequality and disorder more generally, though, it is now appropriate to ask whether social capital can also lead to negative returns.

3

A WALK ON THE DARK SIDE

From most of the social capital literature, there shines out a warm glow. Social capital's 'dark side', by contrast, remains largely unknown terrain. Robert Putnam is typically forthright in arguing that, even if there are some risks from negative cooperation, such as the reciprocity found within criminal gangs, creating more social capital will generally 'be good for us' (Putnam 2000: 414). Yet if Putnam is unusually explicit, he is certainly not alone. Overwhelmingly, those who use the concept have tended to emphasise the positive outcomes of social capital. Yet it may be that this emphasis is profoundly damaging to a full understanding of social networks and norms as resources. Social capital can enable individuals and groups to achieve a variety of common goals, many of which may be negative in their consequences for others, either directly (as for the victims of organised crime), or indirectly (as illustrated by the roles of informal norms and networks in underpinning institutional discrimination). This chapter therefore explores evidence of social capital's negative consequences in two respects. First, it explores the possibility that social capital helps reinforce inequality. Second, it considers the part played by social capital in supporting antisocial behaviour.

It needs to be said at the outset that the optimistic view is far from being irrational or unfounded. Social capital does indeed generate benefits for network members, in that it refers to factors which help individuals and groups to cooperate in order to achieve a common goal. The previous chapter explored some areas in which there is strong evidence for just such a positive association. This in turn has led many writers to assume, explicitly or implicitly, that social capital is in and of itself a generally good thing. By focussing on its role in lubricating the wheels of cooperation, they have concentrated largely on its positive consequences, particularly for the individuals or groups concerned directly, but also for the wider society as a whole. And this is not entirely unreasonable. Even if some of the good news stories turn out to be less convincing on close investigation, there are still plenty of public goods behind the headlines. Education, health, crime reduction, safety, prosperity and individual well-being can all be shown to possess a positive association of some kind with social capital. But if social capital gives rise to desirable outcomes, it can also produce social bads. As Alejandro Portes has put it, 'sociability cuts both ways' (Portes 1998: 18).

Social capital's capacity for negative outcomes should not come entirely as a surprise. If it fosters mutual cooperation for the benefit of members, then social capital is in principle as likely to promote cooperation for negative as well as positive ends. Much the same might be said of financial capital and physical capital. Much of Karl Marx's writing about capital in the nineteenth century was concerned with identifying and explaining its negative consequences. From Marx to Naomi Klein, there is a long line of commentators who have pointed out that what is good for the owner of capital can be thoroughly bad for the worker and consumer – and indeed for the wider environment. Why should social capital be any different? At the very least, we need to understand the extent to which all may gain access to its benefits, and it therefore serves as a public good, or, on the contrary, whether groups may control and deny access to its benefits, in which case it may correspond more to what some have called a 'club good' (Performance and Innovation Unit 2002: 12). Bourdieu's usage, as the previous chapter showed, was largely concerned with the way that clubbish types of social capital serve to underpin struggles for status. Moreover, the consequences of social relationships are rarely simple, and their wider unplanned ramifications are often unpredictable. Cooperative actions that benefit the participants may produce undesirable effects for the wider society (to use economic language, it can create negative externalities), and even for participants, in the form of negative spillover effects (unintended and unwanted).

Nor has this negative capacity gone unnoticed by the concept's primary authors. Writing about the Oklahoma City bomber responsible for the worst terrorist attack to hit the USA before 11 September 2001, Robert

Putnam reflected that Timothy McVeigh had discussed tactics while bowling with fellow right-wing conspirators, concluding that 'just like any other form of capital', social capital can be directed towards malevolent purposes (Putnam 2000: 21–2). He also admitted that inner-city gangs represent forms of social capital, albeit ones where the benefits of solidarity happen to be harmful to bystanders (Putnam 2000: 315–16). But although he was willing to acknowledge that social capital might be misused in certain circumstances, Putnam remained convinced that it was over-whelmingly a force for good. Thus when Putnam devoted an entire chapter in *Bowling Alone* to reviewing the evidence of what he called 'the dark side of social capital', he was really only concerned with whether there was a degree of incompatibility between social capital, equality and freedom. On this specific and very American allegation, Putnam was able to conclude that social capital was innocent on all but a handful of charges (Putnam 2000: 350–63). The links between engagement and democracy are as valid now as when de Tocqueville first proclaimed them.

Fukuyama has also addressed social capital's malign potential. While his original study of the economics of trust took the view that social capital was not just a public good but also for the public good (Fukuyama 1995), he has subsequently recognised the shortcomings of this approach (Fukuyama 2001). He notes that self-interested lobbyists, 'hate groups or inbred bureaucracies' benefit from access to reserves of social capital just as much as anyone. While he also offers examples of negative consequences from physical capital (rifles) and human capital (torture), he concludes that social capital is more likely to produce negative externalities than the other two forms of capital, largely 'because group solidarity in human communities is often purchased at the price of hostility towards out-group members' (Fukuyama 2001: 8). As noted above, trust plays an important role in Fukuyama's concept of social capital, and he explains the negative results of social capital through the idea of the 'radius of trust'. The wider the radius of trust reaches beyond a group's membership, the more benign and positive the externalities; the more the radius of trust is confined to the group's own members, the greater the probability of negative externalities (Fukuyama 2001: 8–10). Nevertheless, Fukuyama believes firmly that although there may be times when there is too much social capital – as, for example, when voluntary organisations produce distortions in public policy – a lack of social capital is far worse (Fukuyama 2001: 12).

It is, then, simply wrong to argue that the founding theorists of social capital have ignored its downside. Indeed, particularly if we pursue

Bourdieu's line of thinking, then the negative consequences of social capital can be seen as inseparable from the benefits. Fukuyama believes that the downside arises from the distribution of trust, which is itself a core element in his definition of social capital. Putnam certainly acknowledges that there are dark consequences, even if these are overwhelmingly outweighed by the benefits. Even Coleman, who was in general far more positive in his views, was aware that social capital might have a downside. Moreover, in principle at least, rational choice theory offers a useful if limited way of understanding the fact that when people cooperate to pursue their own goals, it is sometimes at the cost of others. There is, then, general agreement that social capital might have a dark side. Nevertheless, with the exception of Bourdieu, the leading theorists of social capital have taken a largely benevolent view. If they cannot be convicted of mindless optimism and Panglossian complacency, neither do they sufficiently appreciate the risks inherent in defining social capital as a public good without constant qualification.

SOCIAL CAPITAL AND INEQUALITY

Social capital can promote inequality in large part because access to different types of networks is very unequally distributed. Everyone can use their connections as a way of advancing their interests, but some people's connections are more valuable than others'. As two prominent American commentators have noted,

> Access to social capital depends on the social location of the specific individuals or groups attempting to appropriate it. . . . the social location of the social capital itself affects its 'use value', regardless of who appropriates it.
>
> (Edwards and Foley 1997: 677)

In addition, actors can use their social capital in the way that Bourdieu described, as a means of accessing resources of status and privilege that increase their standing at the expense of others (see also Ledeneva 1998: 125). Furthermore, social capital, according to Bourdieu, is directly useful to network members in its own right, and additionally might help to compensate for shortfalls in respect of other resources. Finally, powerful groups can try to limit or undermine the social capital of those who are less powerful; this was a typical employer strategy in some paternalist industrial communities in the nineteenth century, for instance (Schulman and Anderson 1999). So it is possible to see social capital as both an asset in its own right that is unequally distributed, and as a mechanism that can promote further inequality.

Those who are relatively high on financial and cultural capital also tend to be high on social capital. By this, I mean that they are generally more engaged with other people, and also that their connections tend to be with people who are themselves well connected. All of this may sound heresy to the average Briton, who is used to watching television soaps about working-class communities that are vibrant, diverse and well connected. Yet a British study of participation in a range of leisure activities, ranging from watching sports and attending the cinema to voluntary activity and evening classes, showed a very clear and powerful gradient of involvement. The authors also found similar results when it came to membership of formal associations. They accordingly concluded that: 'Being male, being white, having more education, being of a higher social class, having greater personal income and having more educational qualifications all significantly increased the likelihood of membership of more organisations' (Warde and Tampubolon 2002: 163). Men belong to more organisations in Germany, and are far more likely to hold honorific and leadership positions (Heinze and Strünck 2000: 190). In the USA, survey data have shown that levels of trust are much higher among the well-educated and the rich than among high school dropouts and the poor (Glaeser *et al.* 2000: 815). Similar gaps exist between different ethnic groups: one analysis of responses in the GSS showed that 44.2 per cent of Whites were likely to say that 'most people can be trusted', as against 16.1 per cent of Blacks and 26.6 per cent of individuals from other races (Glaeser *et al.* 2000: 816). Similar findings in other countries confirm this picture (Murtagh 2002; Heinze and Strünck 2000). Volunteering and trust appear to be characteristics of the highly qualified and the middle class.

Yet while levels of engagement may generally be higher among the affluent and educated, this pattern is not entirely unbroken. US survey data tend to suggest that overall associational membership levels among American Blacks are higher than among Whites, largely because of the high rates of religious affiliation among African-Americans (Glaeser *et al.* 2000: 818). Yet while this may give African-Americans a large number of connections, these rarely reach out to members of other ethnic groups, and this can therefore limit the value of the social capital that people can access and operationalise.

Even those organisations that exist in order to represent the disenfranchised, and recruit overwhelmingly among their ranks, often find it
easier to draw in the more prosperous and skilled. Trade union membership
rates tend to be higher among skilled than unskilled workers, while
working-class political bodies such as Britain's Labour Party tend to recruit
disproportionately from groups such as schoolteachers and local government
officers (Seyd and Whiteley 1992). So at the most obvious and simplistic
level, access to the benefits of social capital is unequally distributed.

Yet this is not all the story. Those who have the most connections tend
to use them to advance their interests, and this in turn is a cause of further
inequality. Middle-class families in Britain, and no doubt elsewhere,
systematically use their own connections to advance their children's
education (Allatt 1993). Sztompka's work on Polish elites has shown
that access to networks ranks high as a success factor for the rich and
influential, and is second only to education among the factors that he
studied (Sztompka 1999: 130). Bourdieu, who saw social capital as a
property of privileged groups alone, thought that it could have particular
importance in determining the position within the elite strata of individuals
and groups whose financial capital alone was relatively modest. To give one
example, he argued that members of the professions (above all lawyers and
doctors) often enjoyed middling incomes, but invested systematically in
their children's education and in cultural symbols of 'the bourgeois style
of life', which in turn helped guarantee the value of their social capital.
For this group, he argued, social capital was 'a capital of honourability and
respectability' which could be essential in attracting 'clients in socially
important positions, and which may serve as currency, for instance, in a
political career' (Bourdieu 1977: 503). For Bourdieu, then, social capital
was really a superior form of mutual back-scratching and self-advancement.
It was entirely positive for network members, but served to bolster and
reproduce inequality and privilege in the wider world.

Bourdieu was concentrating on a particularly obvious case of social
capital's contribution to inequality. A slightly more subtle example comes
in a widely cited study of gender bias in the treatment of applications for
post-doctoral research grants in Sweden (Wennerås and Wold 1997). Under
Sweden's Freedom of Information legislation, Christine Wennerås and
Agnes Wold applied for access to the reports compiled by review panels for
the Medical Research Council, and analysed the fate of 114 applications (62
from men, 52 from women). Overall, the panels rated applications from
women below those from men in respect of their scientific competence, the

relevance of the proposed research, and the quality of the proposed method-ology. Wennerås and Wold were then able to compare these results with the research standing of the applicants, which they judged on the basis of the measurable quality of their publications. Their findings demonstrated that women scientists had to appear over twice as often in high status publica-tions as men in order to be considered equally competent by the MRC's reviewers. Wennerås and Wold then examined in detail those characteristics of the applicants which they believed might explain these results, including their field, previous education, prior experience, and whether or not they had declared an affiliation with a panel member. Of all these factors, the only one which appeared to affect the reviewers' opinion was connections between reviewers and applicants, even though the declaration of an affiliation meant that the reviewer was precluded from considering that proposal. Remarkably, this factor appears to have explained virtually the whole of the gender bias, in that the success rates for applicants where an affiliation was declared were the same as for those of male applicants over females.

Wennerås and Wold's research demonstrates the way in which people's connections can both exclude outsiders and allow network members to advance one another's interests. When network self-interest is deliberate (as in Bourdieu's examples), the result is more or less tantamount to nepotism. When based on tacit and habitual use of connections (as in Wennerås and Wold's study), the outcomes are less obviously biased, in that they appear to be generated by the way that particular institutions function, with bias being produced unintentionally, rather than as the result of the individual preferences of network members. Similar processes led Lord Macpherson, in his inquiry into the murder of the young black Londoner Stephen Lawrence, to conclude that the conduct of the police investigation was influenced by institutional racism (Younge 1999). An experimental study of trusting behaviour also found that people were much more likely to base their actions on trust when they believed they were dealing with members of the same ethnic group as themselves (Glaeser *et al*. 2000). By implication, then, people may be less likely to adopt trust-based behaviour when dealing with members of another ethnic grouping.

This raises important questions about the relationship between ethnicity and social capital generally. For example, one commentator has pointed out that Putnam's high social capital states are ethnically homogeneous, and internationally four of the six countries with the highest levels of social capital are Scandinavian. By contrast, the most heterogeneous states and nations (such as Brazil) tend to be low on social capital (Glaeser 2001: 392).

This is not at all to suggest either that there is something genetic about the tendency to be connected, nor that ethnic purity is a prerequisite of connectedness. Rather, as Misztal has pointed out, people tend to feel more confident about predicting the behaviour of people who are like themselves better than they can anticipate the behaviour of people who are different (Misztal 1996: 133–5). This promotes community and reciprocity within ethnic groupings, and can be used to foster cooperation, as among refugees and immigrants but also of course among dominant groups. As people's connections tend to come overwhelmingly from a similar ethnic background to their own (James 2000), it seems highly likely that strong networks often help to promote racial inequality.

Nor is there any shortage of evidence as to the way in which people who are disadvantaged by economics and education can sometimes be held back because of their connections. This is not just a matter of being less engaged, important though that may be as a cause of inequality. The least privileged also tend to have networks which are made up of people in a similar situation to themselves, who are therefore of only limited use in accessing new resources. Data from the Social Change and Economic Life Initiative in mid-1980s Britain show that around a quarter of unemployed people but only 3 per cent of people with jobs said that at least three-quarters of their friends were themselves out of work; moreover, this pattern held good for areas where the labour market was generally buoyant, as well as in areas where unemployment was more common (Russell 1999: 213).

To some extent, of course, people facing tough circumstances can and do find their social capital a useful resource. Adversity can help strengthen bonds, particularly among those who face similar experiences of exclusion or danger. Yet while dense and localised networks may well be very homogeneous and close, because they do not include many people who come from very different backgrounds they tend to give little access to others who could help bring benefits that are situated or controlled outside the community. A study of a housing estate in West Belfast in the later stages of the Troubles showed very high levels of homogeneity among the residents, and relatively little movement into or off the estate. There were 'strong family structures and institutions such as Catholic schools and a Catholic church which reinforced traditional family values' (Leonard 1998: 55), as well as a high level of involvement in the informal economy. Few of the residents were in waged work in the formal economy, and many of the men were registered as unemployed. Icelanders have the saying *hiemskt er heimaalid barn*, which can be translated as 'Stupid is the home-raised child'.

Others have shown similar network characteristics among disadvantaged groups elsewhere. Zhao, in a study of laid-off workers in China, found that typically they had distinctive networks, which were stronger on kinship ties than those of the population at large, but were also lower on the range of resources that were accessible (Zhao 2002: 563). While it seems that Black Americans receive higher returns on their social capital in acquiring employment relative to Whites, this suggests that their opportunities are constrained by racial discrimination and not that their social capital is inherently of greater value; on the contrary, their reliance on intra-ethnic friendships tends to constrain the opportunities that they can access (Aguilera 2002: 869). Black Americans are more likely to call on friends during times of trouble, while Whites are more likely to rely on family (Boisjoly *et al*. 1995: 619). Differences in network characteristics help explain the varying performance of male and female entrepreneurs; women were disadvantaged by the relatively narrow and homogeneous quality of their networks, which restricted the range of sources of information to which they had access (Renzulli *et al*. 2000). An American study of Asian-owned firms showed that although business heads could benefit from their social capital, both in building a market and finding labour among their ethnic communities, those which relied most heavily on social capital were likely to show low income and high failure rates, while those who could access extra-communal resources showed higher incomes and greater longevity (Bates 1994: 686). Georgian and Armenian migrants in post-communist Moscow quickly find work through mutual acquaintances in ethnic group networks, but are then limited to a narrow set of employment opportunities (Stephenson 2001: 537).

Social isolation can of course help reinforce other sources of relative disadvantage. However, it is often impossible to isolate cause and effect in a simplistic manner. One North American study, based on 3,311 interviews, reported that neighbourhood poverty itself did not lead to social isolation; however, it did note declining access to support networks among older respondents and the less well-educated (Boisjoly *et al*. 1995: 623). Network disadvantages also tend to affect disabled people, who are much less likely to be employed, often know fewer other people who are in work, and are more likely to depend on welfare benefits than the population at large. They also suffer direct discrimination as a result of other peoples' attitudes towards disability. Lack of social capital in this case is probably in the end a consequence of prejudice, which leads to denial of employment which in turn places disabled people in a benefits trap, where they can only claim welfare if they prove they are unable to work (Heenan 2002: 385–7). Yet network disadvantage – that is, a lack of ties to people who are already in jobs and might help find an opportunity to escape the benefits trap – is clearly a further source of disadvantage for disabled people whose desire for work is being denied.

This pattern has a number of consequences. High levels of homogeneous social capital represent a strategy for communal survival, without much impact on the wider situation. Where there are externally controlled agencies that have local outlets or centres, and which enjoy considerable respect, they become very important resources, as is shown by the levels of school attainment among the young. In the West Belfast case described above, churches and schools have traditionally enjoyed precisely this type of esteem in the local community, and school attainment levels tend to be much higher than might be expected, given the relatively disadvantaged socio-economic circumstances. Otherwise, high levels of homogeneous social capital are accompanied by virtually no linkages to resources outside the community. By contrast with the West Belfast estate described above, middle-class socialising in Northern Ireland is much more likely to involve settings which bring together people from different backgrounds and communities, enabling access to a much wider range of resources than is available in working-class neighbourhoods (Murtagh 2002: 3). While this is certainly not the only factor at work, it can help make it extremely difficult to secure longer-term changes in the community's position.

A group may find that its capacity to grow its social capital is limited or constrained in some way. For example, women managers are much less likely than men to be given international assignments, which in turn affects the scope of their networks (Caligiuri *et al.* 1999: 163–4). Black Americans who are individually successful in their careers face considerable challenges in acquiring a new stock of social capital that might help them in their new position, since there are proportionately fewer same-race colleagues to serve as sources of support (James 2000: 497).

Further, it has also been suggested that social capital contributes to inequality by exerting a levelling-down effect on people's aspirations (Portes 1998; Harper 2001: 12; Ledeneva 1998: 82). Portes suggests that when group solidarity is cemented by a shared experience of adversity and opposition to mainstream society, then individual members will be discouraged from trying to leave and join 'the enemy'. Group norms then serve to level ambitions downwards, so that the oppressed group keeps its members in a state of continued subjection, and deviant individuals feel impelled to leave the group entirely. Northern Ireland provides an example of this process, where education among the young is promoted vigorously as a means of ensuring local employment, but ambition in adult life is discouraged in order to limit late emigration (Field and Schuller 2000). At the most extreme, those who breach group solidarity may be subjected to violence, as in the case of Roman Catholic youths in Northern Ireland who apply for places in the Police Service or Prison Service. More commonly, though, people are under a constant but subtle pressure not to 'break ranks'.

Similar pressures may explain low levels of participation in community networks and voluntary organisations among disadvantaged groups. Among Afro-Caribbeans in London, for example, levels of informal networking are strong, but it has been suggested that the construction of certain ethnic identities – within a context of institutionalised racism at both the material and symbolic levels – makes it unlikely that people will view local community organisations or networks as representative of their interests or needs, or be motivated to participate in them (Campbell and McLean 2002). Yet their non-participation virtually guarantees that the community's needs are ignored. Again, it has to be emphasised that downward pressures on aspirations are often ignored by able individuals or ambitious organisations. Nor do these pressures function without other, equally significant factors such as a history of discrimination and poverty, which lend legitimacy to attempts to keep aspirations down.

Finally, people hand on their networking skills to their children, which then perpetuates inequality through the generations. In a study of middle-class families in Britain which drew on Bourdieu's model of social capital, Pat Allatt has shown how parents tried to teach their children to acquire a high level of social literacy, and encouraged them to access critical networks (Allatt 1993: 154–7). The parents believed that this would help their children to exercise greater choice and control in their adult lives, so that as well as passing on valuable skills, they were also sharing their insights into the value of connections.

This discussion of social capital and inequality should have confirmed that networks can help to sustain privilege and underpin disadvantage. It would be simplistic in the extreme to suggest that social capital is the only factor involved, or that it is necessarily the most significant. It is even impossible to claim that the best-connected always make use of their network resources to improve their position. Sometimes they do not need to do so, as their other resources can meet their needs. In a study of job search among laid-off workers in China, Zhao found that those with the highest levels of social capital (measured in terms of breadth of networks and the scope of the resources these embodied) were least likely to make use of it, as this group also had the highest levels of human capital, and they were therefore most successful in using formal procedures to find work (Zhao 2002: 566). In post-Soviet Russia, it has even been found that the affluent middle class are disinvesting in established networks, because they no longer have much use for them; goods and services can now be purchased, rather than exchanged. Sarah Busse compares patterns of social capital in Russian cities today with that found in US ghettos, with high closure, multiplexity and continuity but few ties reaching out to those who have resources lacking in one's own group (Busse 2001). So social capital is far from being the dominant factor in creating inequality. Just as people use a mix of different types of resources – including connections – to achieve their goals, so a variety of inequalities tend, in different ways, to reinforce one another. Nevertheless, to return to Bourdieu's metaphor of the casino (page 14), connections are one of the chips at people's disposal, and they can be played when the time seems right.

There are, moreover, at least two types of inequality involved in respect of social capital. First, it has been shown that the most affluent and well-educated are also generally those with the largest number of connections. Second, though, there are also qualitative differences in the nature of people's networks. Indeed, one important question about a person's, community's, or organisation's social capital is to ask whether a particular tie or network is oriented toward providing institutional support; whether the resources accessed are high-quality ones; and the degree to which the support is tailored to need (Stanton-Salazar and Dornbusch 1995: 119). The opportunities for support are then closely related to an individual's or group's position in the wider social hierarchy. So while the connection between inequality and connectedness is not a simple one, there is considerable evidence that both the overall level and the more specific nature of people's social capital can play an important part in determining whether they can access resources. Yet this insight into the influence of social capital on inequality is not a widely discussed one, and it has rarely so far penetrated the discourse of policy-makers.

THE PERVERSE EFFECTS OF SOCIAL CAPITAL

Sociability, as ever, does indeed cut both ways. As well as cooperating for purposes that are generally beneficial both to network members and to others, people can exploit their social capital for purposes that are socially and economically perverse. Of course, definitions of perversity will vary. Many people view Northern Ireland's paramilitaries as terrorists, while their families and neighbours see them as brave freedom fighters; equally, someone who is called a terrorist in Belfast can themselves deplore the doings of Osama Bin Laden. In the same way, armed gangsters in South African shack settlements have been said to help keep down antisocial behaviour among young men, and even promote the use of condoms among sex workers (Campbell 2000: 194). This is said not to sniff over an imagined hypocrisy, but simply to warn that perversity partly exists in the eye of the beholder. Nevertheless, a reasonably clear distinction can be drawn between productive social networks, which we might define as those that generate favourable outcomes both for members and the community at large, and perverse networks, which we could describe as those that have positive benefits for their members but include negative outcomes for the wider community.

This section is concerned primarily with those cases where the perversity is an intentional goal of the network, and only secondarily with those where it is an unintended by-product of its existence. It is easy to think of examples. The most frequently cited is probably organised crime, but there are plenty of others. It is well known that rape is often carried out by people who are already connected with the victim, who can then exploit the connection to ensure that nothing is ever officially reported (Muram *et al*. 1995). Adult sexual gratification networks exist largely in order to exploit such groups as children and people from poor countries (Stephenson 2001: 537). People who belong to networks of injection drug users are much more likely to engage in risky injection practices than those who shoot up alone (Lovell 2002). Fukuyama holds that trust has a general value in easing economic cooperation and reducing the transaction costs associated with more formal mechanisms such as contracts, hierarchies and bureaucratic rules (Fukuyama 2001: 10), but precisely these features of social capital represent an opportunity for those who wish to engage in fraud. And while pluralistic democracy may require a healthy variety of associations, not all associations produce trust in strangers and thus build tolerance and reciprocity at societal level. Some associations are little more than cliques of like people who seek to pursue their own vested interests (Streeck 1999). And so on.

The negative properties of networks have long been known among social scientists. Group identification can also involve stereotyping of outsiders, with damaging consequences. Steven Durlauf cites the results of an experiment by Muzafer Sherif and his colleagues, first published in 1961, which showed that group formation produced rivalry with other groups, along with negative stereotypes which legitimated hostile behaviour bordering on violence (Durlauf 2002: 475). The general assumption that social bonds are good is, Durlauf concludes, an error.

As well as serving to achieve aims that can be widely perceived as undesirable or worse, perverse social capital is often sustained by methods that are themselves widely viewed as illegitimate, such as 'the use of force, violence and/or illegal activities' (McIlwaine and Moser 2001: 968). In a study of the two Latin American nations of Guatemala and Colombia, McIlwaine and Moser (2001: 975) note that a 'significant minority of all social organisations' generated benefits only for their own members and perpetrated violence on others. These included guerrilla and paramilitary groups, neighbourhood gangs, vigilantes and drug cartels; an estimated one in every five membership organisations, almost all male-dominated, was involved in violence.

One possibility is that social capital may form part of a stable system of negative externalities. This hypothesis has been explored by Mark E. Warren with respect to political corruption (Warren 2001). He describes the Antioquia region of Colombia as characterised by a strong system of social networks, based on the family but open to outsiders, combined with strong shared values (which favour work, thrift and strict moral codes) and high levels of trust. It was in this region, with what appears to be a high level of productive social capital, that the Medellin drugs cartel was born, benefiting from the trust relationships among shipping partners to bring cocaine into the export markets of the world. However, Warren also notes that the Colombian political system lacks a set of functioning democratic and juridical institutions, and suggests that the Italian case, if more complex, is also more constructive. Here, corrupt exchanges are facilitated by mutual membership of voluntary associations such as Freemason lodges, which provide ready-made insider networks and serve to constrain disruptive behaviour (for example, 'overcharging' on bribes). By contrast, in Soviet Russia the whole purpose of *blat* networks was to facilitate an economy of favours through personal connections, in a system where monetary exchanges – including bribery – simply did not work (Ledeneva 1998: 39).

Even in the case of the violent Colombian drugs gangs, not all outsiders regard these violent groups as lacking in legitimacy. While 82 per cent of

Colombians were reported as viewing them unfavourably, 18 per cent reportedly trusted them. Of course, this may be associated with relatively low levels of trust in state agencies such as police and judiciary (McIlwaine and Moser 2001: 979). In such cases, it is not only violence that helps maintain perverse social capital. At least as important is the role of fear, sustained by folk tales of particularly memorable acts of violence. In addition, though, perverse social capital also has an up-side, which for network members can be really quite significant. For members of these groups, the benefits were substantial; as well as self-efficacy and a sense of identity, the members were having fun (McIlwaine and Moser 2001: 977). In a turbulent and risky environment, young men in particular found a survival mechanism through perverse organisations. Similar patterns of perverse sociability are found in Moscow among street gangs, which offer a form of social protection to marginal youth in a situation where formal structures – including the family – have often collapsed (Stephenson 2001: 540). And of course, we should not forget the affective dimension to relationships. For some young males, violent gangs are the only network where they encounter people that they like, and who in turn like them.

The gender dimension of perverse social capital is very marked. Organised crime remains a largely male preserve, particularly at leadership level. Most organised gangs are predominantly male; even the all-female *Chicas Big* of Santa Cruz del Quiché, Guatemala, are recruited only from the girlfriends of male gang members, and most of their activities are in support of their boyfriends (McIlwaine and Moser 2001: 977). Indeed, it has been widely recognised that many of the organising principles of adolescent gangs are based on power and the subjection of women. This may currently be changing, as in recent years there has been growing recognition of girls' involvement in youth gangs, and particularly of their role in violence. Yet whereas similarities exist in both their behaviour and their reasons for joining, gang girls report greater social isolation from family and friends, and also lower levels of self-esteem, than the boys (Esbensen *et al*. 1999). There is also a link between perverse social capital and ethnicity, albeit a complex one. Most obviously, trust is higher where similarity is greatest, and perceptions of a criminal threat are often directed against ethnic others (Chiricos *et al*. 2001). Criminal groups are frequently organised along ethnic lines. Sometimes, there is even an explicit commitment to racism and sectarianism. For example, gang members in Moscow are required to swear allegiance to the group's cause, which embraces both criminal activity and extreme nationalism and racism (Stephenson 2001: 540). The use of networks to secure antisocial goals, then, tends to be dominated by males, but not exclusively so. While it is certainly not dominated by a particular ethnic group, ethnicity can be a factor in ensuring the network's homogeneity.

So far, the discussion has concentrated on the use of networks for intentionally perverse goals. Yet there can also be unintended perverse effects as a result of network membership. These arise where the network members are intent on cooperating for a particular purpose, which they may or may not achieve, but find that they have also produced effects that they had not originally bargained for, and possibly did not desire. In Soviet Russia, *blat* networks meant securing a favour that was almost always given at the expense of unknown others; while people denied misconduct in their own case, or saw *blat* as hurting only abstractions like the state, they certainly recognised that other people's use of *blat* was harmful (Ledeneva 1998: 35–6). But perverse effects are just as widespread in capitalist society. Thus the authors of a study on the role of social capital in stimulating knowledge transfer and business innovation in the Nordic economies acknowledge that the same trust-based relations can also create the risk of 'lock-in' to existing strategies and techniques. In this case, employers find they are pushed into holding on to an activity long after it has ceased to have economic value (Maskell *et al.* 1998: 49). Cartel-like behaviour can similarly lead to lower productivity. Business people who socialise with one another are able to turn their competitive rivalry into a basis for cooperation in order to avoid bidding wars and keep up prices (Ingram and Roberts 2000). Yet this then reduces the impact of competition on business behaviour, and insulates employers from the views of customers. Far from stimulating innovation, then, social capital can sometimes produce stagnation and inefficiency.

A parallel process can take place in the political sphere, where engagement in consultative political processes can be dominated by small groups of community leaders. In these cases, the community leaders are able to use their own extensive networks to ensure that others are excluded, or their views discounted as illegitimate. Thus well-established community development associations have at times dominated local regeneration initiatives, to the exclusion of others from local communities (Bockmeyer 2000: 2418). Leadership structures can readily become entrenched in a system of petty (or even not so petty) bosses (Portes and Landolt 2000: 546).

Are perverse results the outcome of a particular type of social capital? This question has been around since the 1950s, when the American anthropologist Edward Banfield used the term 'amoral familism' to explain the behaviour of peasants in southern Italy, which he saw as the result of strategies aimed solely at improving the immediate family's own short-term position. While this might serve the family well, it undermined all attempts at securing wider cooperation (Banfield 1958). Much debated over the years, Banfield's theory shows some affinities with Putnam's explanation for the economic and political differences between northern and southern Italy. More recently, Putnam has accepted the possibility that some kinds of close, bonding ties may inhibit the formation of the looser, bridging links required to resolve the larger collective problems (Putnam 2002: 362–3). We should therefore consider whether there is some explanation here for the tendency of some kinds of social capital to produce perverse effects.

From the time of Simmel, negative social capital – in the form of racism or religious bigotry – has been widely associated with close ties, or bonding social capital. It has also been associated with a tendency towards particularised trust – that is, a propensity to trust those to whom one is related by kinship or personal acquaintance, or who share membership of a known common grouping such as a church or association. Particularised trust may be partly the product of a risky external environment, where it is prudent not to trust strangers. In such circumstances, excluding outsiders and relying on close ties represents a valuable source of security. Moreover, social capital can only act as a resource where individuals have not only formed ties with others but have internalised the shared values of the group. So, for those who do not share the group's values, the subsequent experience of sanctioning is likely to be found highly oppressive. Many people who emigrate from high-trust societies do so because they feel suffocated by the close and self-monitoring community that surrounds them. At first sight, then, it seems that bonding social capital (combined perhaps with particularised trust) is to blame for social capital's dark side.

There is, moreover, some evidence from research to support this thesis. In his study of refugee settlement in twentieth-century Cyprus, Loizos showed that many families had deliberately and successfully set out to intermarry their children to local people, with results that some experienced 'as coercive, indeed claustrophobic' (Loizos 2000: 139). One study of mental well-being among inner-city residents found that while mental distress was marginally lower for residents with higher levels of bridging social capital, bonding social capital was positively related to higher levels of mental distress, suggesting that engagement may bring costs for the individuals concerned (Mitchell and LaGory 2002). A British study of civic engagement and leisure activity found that, while generally those who took part in most activities also belonged to the largest number of organisations, there were two exceptions: gardening and, even more strongly, do-it-yourself activities (Warde and Tampubolon 2002: 164). In these exceptional cases, both of which are based in the home and might reasonably be seen as either neutral with respect to ties or linked primarily with immediate family membership, there was little or no positive association with civic engagement.

Not all the evidence points to such a straightforward model. Bonding social capital – clannishness, the use of family connections – is frequently associated with such public goods as raising educational attainment, reducing the costs of job search and minimising risks of malfeasance in business exchanges. A study of agricultural traders in Madagascar found little evidence of collusion, though it did confirm that social capital helped reduce transaction costs and promoted trust with potential lenders (Fafchamps and Minten 2002). Of course, transactions between people bound by close ties can also go beyond mere mutual back-scratching. Warren suggests that one way of judging such transactions is to ask whether the interests being pursued, and the actions that follow, can be justified publicly (Warren 2001). If the answer is 'yes', then the actions are unobjectionable, and we are simply observing one of the many ways that people get things done in a pluralist society. If the answer is 'no', then it is likely that the actions have gone beyond simply exchanging favours, to embrace some form of behaviour that may have generally damaging consequences for the wider community.

Bridging social capital can also have a dark side. We have already seen that bridging social capital can nurture insider networks and thus reproduce inequality; it may also serve perverse goals. For example, informal networking of highly skilled knowledge professionals was partly responsible for disguising the over-reporting of profits in the 'new economy'. In his study of organised abuse in Italy and Colombia, Warren argues that corruption cannot be ascribed solely to particularised trust (limited to insiders, and usually associated with bonding social capital). In these examples, it also partakes of generalised trust, which can be extended to strangers, albeit usually by means of intermediaries. Warren illustrates his argument with reference to Italian political parties, which provide bridging social capital that brings together government functionaries and business entrepreneurs. For Warren, the decisive factor in determining whether social capital functions positively or negatively for the wider society is its context. His hypothesis is that a context will favour negative social capital when it makes it easier for groups to generate negative externalities, and harder for those subjected to the negative side to resist. This in turn leads Warren to suggest that 'the more political, economic and cultural democracy exists, the less likely sources of social capital with negative potentials are to function in negative ways' (Warren 2001). To some extent, this is another way of saying that inequalities – of power, of resource relationships – matter.

Furthermore, the question of whether social capital has a downside or not may also be a function of the values and lifestyle that a particular community espouses. In a survey study of the links between social capital and sexual health in a South African mining community, it appeared that the impact of associational membership was complicated (Campbell 2000: 194). Levels of HIV infection were lower than average among members of sports groups and churches, but were higher among members of savings clubs, which tend to be associated with high levels of alcohol consumption and sexual promiscuity. It is possible, then, that preferences for a particular type of antisocial behaviour are formed outside the social capital that people then develop in order to pursue that behaviour more rewardingly in the future.

Perhaps it is important not to draw too sharp a distinction between bonding ties and bridging links. It is true that people often choose their engagement in associations and other loose ties, whereas they do not choose their families. People tend to develop bridging ties on the basis of an existing interest or preference; they then seek out others who share the same concerns, and may start joining associations that bring together others still. Bonding ties, on the other hand, include some connections that are not entirely a matter of choice. Whether or not one decides to break with family members whose values and behaviour seem offensive or damaging is at best a constrained choice, even in the most mobile and flexible of social systems. But it is important not to overestimate the degree of choice involved in people's bridging links, nor to underestimate the choice involved in bonding ties. What is clear at this stage is that close ties appear more frequently associated with perverse consequences than more distant ones, but that neither is entirely exempt.

SOCIAL CAPITAL'S DARK SIDE

Of course, social capital is hardly alone in being a resource which may be used for good or for bad. As Fukuyama himself points out, physical capital can take the form of rifles, and a government can invest in the human capital of its official torturers (Fukuyama 2001: 8). Moreover, the Tocquevillian assumption that all civic association is good is not shared universally. Mussolini's fascist movement, for example, involved an extremely high level of engagement by Italian citizens. Equally, well-informed and active citizens may decide not to engage in particular types of civic activity. Criticising Putnam for what they see as excessive concern over falling levels of trust in government in the USA, one group of British political scientists have suggested that low political trust may well be associated with high levels of social capital and education (Maloney *et al.* 2000a: 217). It should now be clear that we cannot see connectedness as invariably positive. Sometimes it can serve negative ends as well as good; and frequently it forms part of a wider structure of systematic inequality.

Social capital as a concept has acquired a high normative charge. Its prevailing image in recent debates has been largely positive, and some of its advocates have tended to ignore evidence that runs counter to their claims. For example, both Fukuyama and Putnam make much of evidence linking social capital with economic performance (Fukuyama 1995; Putnam 2000). Yet China and Italy are also high-growth economies, despite their notoriously low levels of trust and association, while high-trust societies like Germany and Japan are facing major problems in adjusting to the requirements for flexibility and agility of an increasingly globalised capitalism (Misztal 1996: 117). We turn in the next chapter to the question of social capital's relevance in the new social order. We should do so bearing in mind that connections can cut both ways.

4

SOCIAL CAPITAL IN A (POST)MODERN WORLD

The idea that we live at a time of unprecedented change is widespread. For Britain's monarch, marking a half-century on the throne, this was the dominant theme of a lifetime:

> If a Jubilee becomes a moment to define an age, then for me we must speak of change – its breadth and accelerating pace over these years. . . . Change has become a constant.
>
> (Queen Elizabeth II 2002)

These changes are indeed far-reaching and have encompassed many of the areas touched on in this book. The eminent sociologist Manuel Castells has spoken of this as coming together in the rise of a network society, where fixed and direct relationships of all kinds are being replaced by open systems of coordination based on what he calls 'networks of networks' (Castells 1996). Ulrich Beck has a rather different perspective, arguing that we live in an age where the ethic of 'individual self-fulfilment and achievement is the most powerful current in modern society' (Beck 2000: 165). For Beck, the sources of collective identity and meaning which underpinned Western industrial societies – family, national state, ethnicity, class and job – are exhausted and no longer provide for either personal security or social integration. Beck's thesis suggests that 'bowling alone' is simply a by-product of the growth of individualism and the individualisation of social relations. Postmodern conditions may also explain the rising academic and wider interest in social capital. 'Social capital', it has been suggested, 'perhaps matches the spirit of an uncertain, questing age' (Schuller *et al*. 2000: 38). The very insecurity of our own connections in a period of what Kirchhöfer (2000: 15) calls 'the individualised social shaping of the individual' may just be what is drawing our attention to their value.

A brief outline of the areas of change should be sufficient to indicate both their scale and their potential importance for a theory of social capital. Work has become increasingly flexible and adaptable, economic institutions have adjusted to the pressures and opportunities of globalised markets. In much of the world, family structures have been transformed, with exceptionally dramatic changes in the role of women and the elderly. Communism has collapsed, removing at a stroke the one visible socio-economic alternative to capitalism, and helping further to open up world markets to deregulated competition. Information technology in particular, and scientific advance in general, have brought about enormous growth in humanity's capacity for control over its destiny, as well as in its ability to foul it up, generating a pervasive awareness of risk and uncertainty. The penetration of knowledge into all domains of life has created a new openness in the fate of individuals; people have ever greater capacities for self-interpretation and constant reconstruction of their own identity. Anthony Giddens has suggested that the 'reflexive project of the self' is an inescapable fate, involving a continuous refashioning of social life (Giddens 1991). In the context of a more individualised and reflexive citizenry, the nature and meaning of civic engagement must inevitably change as well (Melucci 1996). In short, many of the social coordinates on which people depend are in a process of transformation. This in turn must have consequences for the way in which people can use their relationships as a basis for cooperating and securing their mutual advantage.

At first sight, it is tempting to suggest that connections might lose their importance in a more open and flexible world. Yet it is quite conceivable that the reverse is at least as likely an outcome. After all, it has often been said that informal networks lost much of their importance in the context of modern societies (Rose 1999: 147). Max Weber, the classical sociologist of bureaucratic organisation, contrasted premodern society's reliance on direct interpersonal connections as a source of social solidarity and order with modernity's distinctive reliance on impersonal regulation and bureaucratic organisation. Roles were typified by predictability, order and routine. Weber, though, was writing at the turn of the last century, when mass industrial society was reaching dominance in the Western nations, and imperial systems covered much of the rest of the world. Moreover, he may have underestimated the extent to which informal ties survived modernity, and enabled people to do things despite the myriad rules and elaborate hierarchies that surrounded their lives. Nevertheless, in the late twentieth century, organised routine, large-scale bureaucracy and state regulation were displaced at least in part by what some writers called 'disorganised capitalism' or 'postmodernity'. What is the role of social capital under postmodern conditions? Above all, is it in (possibly terminal) decline – or, on the contrary, are people simply adapting and developing new types of connectedness, alongside their old networks?

These are large questions, and the answers can only be sketched out here. This chapter explores a number of recent changes, and examines the key implications for the concept of social capital. In examining the impact of the networked society, it is essential to consider how the rise of online communication is affecting people's networks. Above all, is the Internet reducing people's reliance on face-to-face interaction, or does it provide a complementary means of communicating? This chapter also examines the collapse of communism, not least because the sharp and sudden transition to democracy after 1989 has virtually created an 'hour zero', where old connections lost much of their value, but new ones were being created in highly uncertain circumstances. The chapter also explores the role of social changes, particularly in intimate and family relationships, on the nature of the connections that people can access. However, the first question to be addressed is the central one of active citizenship. Putnam, it has already been suggested, is a modern-day de Tocquevillian. He is worried about the decline of community in America because he believes that it will damage the health of American democracy. This is such a central concern in the social capital literature that it merits close and detailed attention.

ACTIVE DEMOCRATIC CITIZENSHIP

Since the early 1990s, Putnam has written with particular force about the importance of associational life for American democracy. This reflects a wider preoccupation among political scientists in the USA with the health of the political system at a time when active participation of various types appears to be in decline. One oft-used example is the low proportion of

Americans who choose to vote in presidential elections. It is not surprising that Putnam discusses the decline in American commitment to electoral participation, which he believes to be far sharper and more serious than is indicated by the falling numbers who chose a president (Putnam 2000: 32). Yet if there is widespread concern over people's unwillingness to go out and vote in elections, Putnam's argument is given added impetus by his explicit attachment to the Tocquevillian tradition. As shown above, Alexis de Tocqueville saw a wide range of associational life not only as integral to good government, but also as the robust and durable foundation of a pluralistic society. If this were true, then the long-term decline that Putnam detects in communal association is likely to damage the prospects of good government and social cohesion alike. So is Putnam's anxiety well founded, or not?

Putnam has repeatedly claimed that the USA's aggregate stock of social capital is in decline (Putnam 1993b, 1995, 2000). To support this claim, he has presented evidence that such indicators as rates of joining voluntary associations, levels of trust between individuals, rates of voting, and levels of sociability are all dwindling. To demonstrate that connectedness is falling, Putnam presents evidence from national survey data, the membership records of a variety of organisations, and other measures of volunteering and sociability. Even in the wake of the 11 September events, when Putnam found evidence of a sizeable rise in levels of trust and awareness of politics among Americans, there was no evidence of any recovery in levels of social interaction and volunteering (Putnam 2002). His evidence on this question is certainly detailed, and to some extent it is compelling; it is certainly not consistent with the view that nothing at all has changed. Some other researchers, including scholars who have otherwise been sharply critical of his explanations, have found similar evidence of a considerable decline in national membership organisations in the USA, accompanied by growth in (largely salaried) national-level lobbying and advocacy organisations (Skocpol and Fiorina 1999).

Putnam also considers evidence of changes in people's values. He draws on survey findings to produce evidence of a long-term decline in trust and in trustworthiness. In particular, he has used responses over time to a standard question, routinely asked in the General Social Survey (GSS) undertaken since 1974 by the National Opinion Research Centre at the University of Chicago: 'Generally speaking, would you say that most people can be trusted, or that you can't be too careful in dealing with people?' (Putnam 2000: 137). The same question is used in the World Values

Survey, allowing Putnam and others to compare levels of generalised trust not only over time but between different countries. Over time, Putnam has found a marked fall in levels of trust in the USA, and this is accompanied by very strong cohort effects, with far lower levels of trust among the young and far higher levels among older people (Putnam 2000: 140–1). Again, reworking of the same data by a group of economists, using a multiple regression framework, produced similar results (Glaeser *et al*. 2000: 816–17). So once more, Putnam appears to be presenting a convincing case.

On the basis of this evidence, Putnam concludes that 'most Americans are less connected to our communities than we were two or three decades ago' (Putnam 2000: 180). Yet his claims have proven enormously controversial. Perhaps the most detailed critique has come from Pamela Paxton, who examined much of the same data as Putnam. In a detailed analysis of findings from the General Social Surveys, Paxton tried to examine the extent and nature of change in social capital in the United States between 1975 and 1994. Like Putnam, she also examined patterns of association, and found little sign of change over the period. Of her three indicators of association, the number of memberships stayed steady; time spent socialising with neighbours fell slightly; time spent socialising with friends rose slightly (Paxton 1999: 114–16).

Combining seven indicators for trust (three relating to trust in individuals and four to trust in institutions), Paxton found a small but clear decrease in both types of trust, but with a slightly stronger decline in trust in individuals (Paxton 1999: 112–14). However, Paxton's analysis also showed that levels of trust varied enormously from one year to the next; there was a sharp fall in trust in religion in 1988, presumably as a result of the scandal over the private life of the television evangelist Jim Baker. Trust in political institutions was dragged down by the Watergate scandal and the Iran–Contra affair. Paxton concluded that 'when shocks to trust in institutions related to specific events are allowed in the model, there remains no separate general decline in trust in institutions' (Paxton 1999: 118–19). This is surely a tad optimistic. Scandals do erode trust in public institutions, just as personal betrayal erodes trust in private relationships. If people feel that trusting behaviour is abused, then their propensity to trust accordingly declines. Nevertheless, Paxton is right to remind us that specific events are an important part of the pattern. The question then is whether there are more external shocks to trust than there were in the past. If so, then that might help explain why social capital in America appears to be in decline.

As well as doubts over the alleged decline in aggregate stocks of social capital in the US, there is also controversy over Putnam's account of the changing nature of organisational membership. In regard to civic engagement in the USA, Jean Cohen has described Putnam's picture of decline as resting on 'waning and anachronistic models of civic association', accusing him of screening out newer forms of association (Cohen 1999: 212). Although he recognises the growth of membership in new social movement organisations like Greenpeace and Amnesty International, Putnam describes these as 'tertiary' organisations, in which membership is 'essentially an honorific device for fund-raising' (Putnam 2000: 156). Such 'mail-order members' are not active in the cause and may never meet one another, so that their organisations 'provide neither connectedness among members nor direct engagement in civic give-and-take' (Putnam 2000: 160). Rather than building social capital, they can deplete it by breaking the direct link between civic engagement and social interaction. Yet Putnam is stronger on assertion than evidence; the impact of 'tertiary associations' on social capital has yet to be examined on a systematic basis. Nevertheless, there is some evidence about the views of chequebook participation as seen by the members. One British study suggests that chequebook activists themselves develop a strong level of group identification, and see themselves very much as belonging to a community of like-minded people (Maloney 1999). The question of chequebook activism may, in fact, be analogous to that of online forms of engagement, as will be seen below.

Even if we accept that engagement is declining in the US – and this remains controversial – the American pattern may not be typical. While Putnam's recent work has focussed almost entirely on the USA, he occasionally draws selectively on evidence of similar trends elsewhere to support his argument (for example, in respect of television's malign influence: see Putnam 2000: 236). Yet studies in Europe in particular have tended to suggest that the US might be an exception (albeit a rather significant one). Swedish survey data confirm a steady decline in support for the largest voluntary organisations, and an accompanying rise in individualistic values across all strata of the population. This has been balanced by growing involvement in smaller voluntary organisations and continuing public support for universal welfare programmes (Rothstein 2001: 219–21). National data from Britain do not support the thesis of an overall decline in associational membership (Hall 1999). Rather, they suggest considerable variation between different types of organisations, as well as within them. Most spectacularly, there has been enormous decline in the membership of traditional women's organisations, with equally striking gains among environmental organisations (Hall 1999: 421). Similarly, time-use data in Britain suggest that informal sociability has grown in recent decades (Hall 1999: 427). The most comprehensive study of time-use in Britain suggests that both men and women spend much more time with their children than in the 1960s, and are more likely to spend time socialising; there has also been a huge rise in the time spent playing sports (including bowling) with others, particularly among young women but also among other groups as well (Gershuny and Fisher 1999). So the national UK evidence does not really offer much support to Putnam's hypothesis.

Nor is Putnam's thesis supported by German data. Analysis of data from surveys conducted in the mid-1980s and mid-1990s shows a small but clear growth in the numbers of Germans who were involved in volunteering. This rise took place among all age groups, including the young; it was slightly higher for women than men, leading to convergence between the genders in respect of overall levels of volunteering (Heinze and Strünck 2000: 189–91). According to the same study, though, the pattern of volunteering in Germany was changing, just as it had done in Britain. The numbers who were active in party politics and general political activity were falling, particularly among the young; the largest rise came in what the authors defined as 'irregular' volunteering – that is, occasional rather than routine involvement and in a rapidly expanding group of self-help groups (Heinze and Strünck 2000: 189–91, 202). So, even if most Germans are not flocking to play and serve in organised leagues, neither are they opting to bowl alone.

This finding is also consistent with local studies. One account of associations in Birmingham, England, produced that conclusion that 'there has been a significant increase in civic involvement over the last 30 years and not a precipitous decline' (Maloney *et al.* 2000: 219). Much of the growth came in social welfare associations, educational bodies, youth groups and, above all, churches (this latter can be seen as probably arising from the multicultural nature of the city's population). Several scholars have criticised Putnam for neglecting the role of political institutions (Cohen 1999; Lowndes and Wilson 2001; Maloney *et al.* 2000b; Rothstein 2001), which can directly influence the extent to which voluntary and community groups flourish or decline. So, just as in the case of levels of trust, levels of associational membership can change in response to events.

There is also some evidence in Europe that those who have the highest levels of social (and human) capital are also the most selective when it comes to political participation. Alain Touraine suggests that the demise of the welfare state is closely connected with individualisation, which has witnessed the appearance of new forms of citizenship. Rather than seeking to belong to wider collectivities, they have developed resources which enable them to 'resist the logic of technical objects, instruments of power and social integration' (Touraine 1995: 230). One multi-country study provided evidence of the growth of a group of political 'spectators', who were well educated and highly engaged, and actively interested in political issues, but took the view that they could pursue their own concerns more effectively by other means. For them, direct political engagement was entirely discretionary, and compared with other matters its relevance was relatively low (Van Deth 2000). A German study has pointed to the possibility of greater selectivity in volunteering; people are increasingly inclined to support self-help groups that serve their own particular needs, while highly qualified younger people are turning to voluntary activity as a preparation for entry into a career (Heinze and Strünck 2000: 190, 202). Another German survey, which similarly confirms a general rise in volunteering, notes that traditional types of motivation such as 'helping other people' are increasingly being complemented by a desire for self-realisation through volunteering; out of nineteen different reasons that people gave for volunteering, the most important factor was judged to be 'enjoyment' (Klages 2000: 158–9). As a strategy for securing the common good, then, direct engagement in the political process may be rather on the margin for some otherwise very engaged groups.

When it comes to declining levels of trust, though, American exceptionalism may be less marked. Certainly the British data yield a similar finding to those for the USA: the proportion of Britons claiming that they generally trusted others fell from 56 per cent in 1959 to 44 per cent by 1990. However, it is worth noting that – in distinction to the US – levels of trust dropped among all generations more or less in line with the general trend (Hall 1999: 432). Hall has argued that since this decline in trust occurred over a period when associational membership was buoyant, Putnam's assertion of a close link between the two must be questionable. Rather, it appears that some types of organisation promote trust – particularly those which advance a common cause – while others are dedicated more towards a private interest, and may require little or no face-to-face interaction (Hall 1999: 449).

Putnam particularly blames the long-term decline in American community to the malevolent influence of television. He is unambiguous in condemning the culprit in the corner, describing dependence on TV as '*the single most consistent* predictor that I have discovered' (Putnam 2000: 230; emphasis in original). In the year after 11 September 2001, Putnam noted a significant rise in time spent watching television and a decline in having friends round to visit; he concluded that Americans were 'cocooning' themselves rather than joining political and social movements (Putnam 2002). There are, he believes, three reasons why TV has this disastrous influence on social capital. First, it takes up time that might be used socialising, and keeps people in their home. Second, TV encourages passivity and 'lethargy'. Third, the content of most shows tends to be anti-civic; while people who regularly watch the TV news appear to be more engaged than the population at large, there is a marked negative association between active citizenship and regular viewing of game shows, chat shows and soaps (Putnam 2000: 237–43). Yet if these arguments were correct, then social capital would be suffering similarly wherever TV holds sway. In fact, Putnam's claim that television is the main culprit for civic engagement has attracted widespread criticism even with respect to the US (Uslaner 1999). In Britain, it appears to be entirely implausible. When asked where they had 'learned the most about sex and growing up', only 13 per cent of young Britons mentioned television and radio, while 27 per cent cited their friends and 22 per cent their teachers (Summerskill 2002). Personal connections, in other words, remain strong even among the Big Brother generation of viewers. As Hall has shown, the generations that grew up with TV in Britain do not show lower levels of community involvement than those who grew up between the wars. Although Hall notes evidence suggesting that those who watch most are the least active in community organisations (Hall 1999: 433–4), this is of course as likely to be the result of other factors, since TV viewing is also closely associated with such characteristics as social class, educational level and even region of residence.

If TV is Putnam's main culprit, he also fingers a number of other co-conspirators. Chief among these is the effect of generational change. Putnam's evidence suggests that some changes – particularly the decline in certain types of sociability and organisational membership – may be 'almost entirely' due to generational succession. In particular, he points to the gradual disappearance of a 'long civic generation' of American joiners. This group, born between around 1910 and 1940, went through the Depression and Second World War as central levelling and unifying experiences (Putnam 2000: 254). The subsequent Baby Boomer generation, whose formative experiences took place during the late 1950s and the 1960s and who often express strong beliefs in community, has not in practice provided nearly as many joiners as its parents' and grandparents' generations. Putnam notes that the Boomers were 'the first generation to be exposed to television throughout their lives' (Putnam 2000: 257). They in turn were followed by the Gen-X cohort, who according to Putnam have 'accelerated the tendencies to individualism', and have given up on both formal associational membership organisations and less formal schmoozing types of activity such as entertaining at home, card-playing or family dining (Putnam 2000: 259–66). Once more, though, Putnam's findings in the USA are not mirrored elsewhere. Hall has shown that in Britain, although there initially appears to be a similar association between age and engagement to that reported by Putnam, this breaks down on closer scrutiny. When organisational involvement was compared at given ages, Hall found that those in the Boomer generation tended to belong to at least as many associations at any given age as did the inter-war generation when they were the same age (Hall 1999: 430). There is also evidence from Britain of a growth in informal care networks like baby-sitting circles and school-run car-sharing, largely created by women and arising from the decline of the extended family and continuing increases in labour market participation (Lowndes 2000: 536).

Before leaving this subject, we should also note that some of Putnam's indicators have also been questioned by other scholars. Partly this is a matter of definition, just as is the question of whether trust is best seen as a component or an outcome of social capital (see above, pages 62–5). For example, Paxton suggests that voting might be viewed less as a part of social capital than as an outcome (Paxton 1999: 90). Some of the concerns are more fundamental. In particular, Putnam appears to assume that responses to GSS questions on trust are relatively unproblematic. Glaeser and his colleagues note that responses might vary for a variety of reasons. For example, people may have different interpretations of what it means to trust others, or have different understandings about the meaning of 'most people' (Glaeser *et al.* 2000: 815). Glaeser and his colleagues used an experimental approach to measure trust and trustworthiness, based on the behaviour of individuals when confronted with simple ethical dilemmas; they found that while responses to the standard attitudinal questions had some correlation with the trustworthiness of their subjects, they generally did not predict the choices that their subjects made (Glaeser *et al.* 2000: 826). More generally, it is widely accepted that attitudes and behaviour often do not correspond. Partly this seems to arise because surveys tend to depend on self-reported attitudes, and subjects may be unaware of what they really feel, or may decide to give an untruthful answer. So although it is important to note that overall reported levels of trust in the US and some other countries appear to have declined, it is also important to acknowledge that survey data are at best ambiguous where such a sensitive topic as trust is concerned.

So far as civic engagement is concerned, then, it looks as though the jury should be left in its meeting hall for some time yet. Putnam's claims about levels of community in the USA seem to be relatively strong in respect of civic engagement and informal sociability, but the pattern may not be nearly as uniform as he suggests. In Europe, by contrast, civic engagement and informal sociability both appear to be relatively buoyant. Incidentally, it is worth noting that Putnam recorded a rise in levels of trust among Americans in the twelve months following the terrorist attacks of 11 September 2001; this pattern was, moreover, shared for all age and ethnic groups, with the predictable exception of Arab-Americans who were somewhat less trusted than before (Putnam 2000). So it seems that specific events can have quite a dramatic impact on levels of trust. Putnam's evidence on trust is highly suggestive, and is paralleled by developments in Britain, but as it is drawn from survey evidence that is inherently ambiguous, these findings are far from being conclusive. Rather than a simple decline in communal engagement, then, it seems likely that we are witnessing signs of changes in the ways that people express their engagement.

ATOMISED CONNECTIONS IN CYBERSPACE

Online interaction has expanded at a remarkable rate in recent years. Given the sheer surge in the numbers using online communications, and the rapid spread of uses to which it may be put, it would be surprising if it had no impact on people's social capital. While this did not attract comment from Coleman and Bourdieu, at least to my knowledge, Putnam devoted an entire chapter of *Bowling Alone* to this subject. Although he accepts that the Internet removes barriers to communication and thus facilitates new networks, he remains somewhat sceptical about its influence. In particular, he notes the emerging digital divide between those who are connected and those who lack the skills and equipment to enter cyberspace. Second, because online communication is casual and lacks the instant feedback of face-to-face encounters, it discourages reciprocity and facilitates cheating.

Third, people who go online tend to mix only with small groups of others who share the same interests and views as themselves and they are intolerant of anyone who thinks otherwise. Finally, the Internet offers abundant opportunities for private and passive entertainment. While he warns against early judgement of a technology that is still in its infancy, Putnam believes that ideals of online citizenship face serious challenges (Putnam 2000: 172–7).

In general, there has been much speculation on this subject, but until recently relatively little hard evidence. One of the most celebrated prophets of postmodernity, Francis Fukuyama, has argued that digital technologies themselves are inimical to the creation of social capital. According to Fukuyama,

> when the information age's most enthusiastic apostles celebrate the breakdown of hierarchy and authority, they neglect one critical factor: trust, and the shared ethical norms that underlie it.
>
> (Fukuyama 1995: 25)

Fukuyama is by no means alone in believing that the Internet erodes established relationships. According to Manuel Castells, the eminent Catalan social theorist, the new technologies have helped demolish the rigid identities of industrial modernism, based on class and nation, so that we now live in a network society where all kinds of contacts and values can be built into our sense of who we are. For Castells, the new technologies are central to this process of opening up the social space, for they provide unparalleled opportunities for linking disparate and scattered elements into a fluid but structured whole. His examples reflect the ambiguities of the new order: they include drug trafficking cartels, intergovernmental agencies, street gangs, global media corporations, finance houses and online ethnic diasporas (Castells 1996; see also Turkle 1997: 177–89).

For most of the Internet's brief life, evidence on the relationship between social capital and online connectivity has been hard to come by. Yet even in the period since Putnam completed *Bowling Alone*, a number of studies have been published which allow us to examine both his hypotheses and those of Castells and Fukuyama. Very broadly, they seem to suggest that those who develop connections through the Internet are neither devious individualists nor the shock troops of hypermodernity. Most survey-based evidence shows that those who are most active online tend to be people who already have plenty of face-to-face connections, and they complement rather than replace these by interaction in cyberspace (Wellman 2001: 2032).

Table 4.1 Civic engagement among Internet users and non-users

	Internet users (%)	Non-users (%)
Human rights	63	72
Sports club	47	43
Environmental action	61	71
Politics	35	25
Church	18	28

Source: Kniep 2000: 21

The first large-scale survey of Internet use in Germany showed that intensive users were less likely than non-users to be involved in churches, human rights groups and environmental action but more likely to be involved in politics and sports (see Table 4.1). Rather than representing a breed of cyber-isolates, then, German Internet users simply had different types of involvement from non-users. They were also less likely to value the family as 'specially important' than non-users and more likely to envisage living as a single person (Kniep 2000: 21, 23). They watched less television than non-users, and spent less time sleeping. Internet users also believed that they spent less time reading than non-users, but in fact they turned out to spend significantly more time reading (Kniep 2000: 27). The author of this study concluded that Internet users were, in general, 'more egotistical' and less patient than non-users, but he was unable to say which was cause and which was effect (Kniep 2000: 21).

Kniep's findings are consistent with other studies of Internet usage. A survey of visitors to the National Geographic Society website found that heavy Internet use was generally associated with high levels of participation in voluntary organisations and political associations; they also found a generally positive association between online interaction and offline participation (Wellman *et al.* 2001). In their detailed investigation into Internet use and civic engagement in Britain, Jonathon Gardner and Andrew Oswald produced similar results (Gardner and Oswald 2002). Drawing on data from the Social Attitudes Survey, Gardner and Oswald found no difference between Internet users and non-users in levels of trust, but there were marked if small-scale differences in sociability. Against their expectations, Gardner and Oswald found that Internet users were more likely to be involved in social and voluntary organisations than non-users, and were even more likely to attend church. They also tended to rely more on friends and less on family than non-users (a pattern that persisted after allowing for age and other factors). Interestingly, given Putnam's hypothesis, they also watched quite a lot less television. Gardner and Oswald conclude that, in Britain, the Internet is not contributing to a decline in social capital.

Similar findings have emerged from other methods, though as yet genuine longitudinal studies are rare (Wellman 2001: 2032). Jonathan Gershuny has drawn largely comparable conclusions from a series of time-use studies. Gershuny illustrated his findings by showing that when controlling for other relevant variables (such as the likelihood of being in employment among web users), each extra minute a day spent on the Internet is associated with less time spent watching television, less time spent on personal care, and a little less on visiting other people, but also rather more time spent on going out; the increase in sociability was particularly marked among new Internet users (Gershuny 2001). Perhaps surprisingly, studies of online networks show that while the proportionate gain in contact is greatest for connections living at a distance, online and offline contact are both greatest with those living nearby (Wellman 2001: 2033). Thus the Internet allows both the proliferation of weak ties and the maintenance of spatially distant strong ties (Wellman and Hampton 1999).

Most of the quantitative evidence, then, seems to support the view that online interaction complements face-to-face engagement, and may even supplement it. However, this needs to be qualified in at least two ways. First, most of the findings come from a straightforward statistical analysis of survey data, and they do not tell us *why* online interaction and face-to-face community are associated. The possibility remains that both arise from other factors – the fact, for example, that both Internet users and civic participants tend to be relatively well-educated, and tend to enjoy relatively high income levels. We know from other research that these two variables are associated with good access to personal networks. Aggregate data may also need to be broken down, as the possibility remains that intensive Internet use is not compatible with the idea of spending time on face-to-face encounters. An American study of website users revealed that, while most Internet users were generally prone to civic engagement, the very heaviest users were not particularly committed, and did not even share the idea and practice of online community (Wellman *et al*. 2001). So there may be some exceptions to the generally positive association between online interaction and face-to-face engagement.

Second, we still do not know just what wider consequences follow from online interaction. Of course, there is a lot of speculation and gossip, for example about online interaction and adultery, but this is as yet a poorly researched area. There is no real evidence on the type of social capital that is being produced by networks of online networks. It seems sensible, then, to assume that online relationships may have different effects from those produced through face-to-face interaction. This is certainly the view of Barbara Misztal, who claims that co-presence plays an important role in reducing ambiguity of communication and increasing mutual knowledge, while physical absence can help overcome the limitations of close, localised ties (Misztal 2000: 135–6). In respect of dense networking, Urry argues that virtual interaction rarely substitutes for 'corporeal travel', since 'inter-mittent co-presence' appears to be essential for some types of social interaction to flourish, particularly those which give rise to social capital (Urry 2002).

Perhaps the most persuasive analysis of the meanings of virtual sociality is that of Sherry Turkle. Based on many years of observation and direct participation in gaming and other online communities, Turkle draws striking conclusions about the relationship between interaction in cyber-space and reflexivity of the self: 'When we step through the screen into virtual communities, we reconstruct our identitities on the other side of the looking glass' (Turkle 1997: 177). She suggests that the Internet serves as a 'significant social laboratory for experimenting' with self-identity, particularly where people are able to take on and build a quasi-fictional character and work through the consequences of their choices, as in the MUDs (multi-user domains) used by gaming groups (Turkle 1997: 180–4). Even so, she argues, the possibilities offered by virtual experiences are relatively shallow ones; her studies of gender-swapping lead her to conclude that some people are encouraged to believe that they have achieved greater depth of identity change than is in fact the case (Turkle 1997: 238). Thus, the best available evidence suggests that people who interact online are already doing just what Urry suggests. In so far as they are creating and building their social capital, it is likely to be qualitatively different than that which is created by face-to-face interaction.

At this stage, it seems that there is no real basis in principle for viewing online interaction and face-to-face relationships as incompatible. The Internet is not as yet demonstrably harming people's social capital. Rather, it seems to be complementing it, and allowing them to extend their existing networks in ways that enrich and build upon their face-to-face connections. Yet neither does the evidence suggest that the Internet is the basis for an entirely new form of active citizenship. If they are helping to open up the social space in the ways that Castells prophecies, they are doing so unevenly and incrementally rather than in huge bounds. Rather than seeing the Internet as somehow marking a completely new departure, which may be destroying existing reserves of social capital, it may be better to view it as one of many factors which are eroding some types of social solidarity (noticeably those based on workplace, neighbourhood and immediate kinship bonds) and promoting a turn to more openly bounded, loosely knit and provisional forms of engagement. In so far as it may be helping to shift people's interactions away from those based on 'ascribed' characteristics such as gender, class or age, and towards 'achieved' characteristics such as common lifestyles or hobbies (Wellman and Hampton 1999), the Internet is therefore very much at one with those wider changes that are – in Giddens' words – promoting reflexivity of the self.

THE END OF COMMUNISM

In 1989, writing when the Berlin Wall was still unchipped, Francis Fukuyama spoke in a public lecture of the collapse of communism as the end of history (Fukuyama 1989). Perhaps understandably in that heady summer, Fukuyama's language was hyperbolic. It was also profoundly conservative, effectively celebrating the triumph of economic as well as political liberalism. Yet Europe was witness to a remarkable transformation in 1989, whose implications have been far-reaching. Strangely, the collapse of European communism has been strangely neglected in discussions of postmodern social formations. Once under way, the process was astonishingly rapid, and the insertion of the former communist nations into relatively unregulated market capitalism has been virtually complete.

In the process of replacing state regulation of distribution virtually overnight by an extreme and sometimes corrupt form of free market capitalism, one might have predicted a massive deflationary loss in the value of existing social capital. Many of the decisions of everyday life under communism may have been eased considerably by the use of connections. In her study of the 'economy of favours' in Russia, Ledeneva points out that *blat* (the systematic use of connections to procure favours) was originally a response to the absence of a market; having money was largely irrelevant when it came to getting hold of everyday goods such as food, clothing or a home (Ledeneva 1998: 35). Whether or not *blat* involved powerholders in the regime, or the more mundane use of family and friends and then friends of friends to find scarce goods, their value was closely tied to the circumstances imposed by the state's monopoly on power, which affected private life as much as the economy. Given the pace of integration into Western capitalism, it seems logical to suppose that all social institutions, at all levels, would be affected – and would, in their turn, also shape the nature of Central European capitalism. The question is therefore a dual one: what has been the role of social capital in this remarkable transition – and how have the changes impacted upon social capital?

A number of scholars have sought to use the concept of social capital to shed light on the societies of post-communist Europe. Kolankiewicz draws on both Putnam and Bourdieu as authorities for his analysis of class formation in Poland and Hungary, countries where communism was always extremely unpopular, and where the regime was therefore required to reach some sort of accommodation with the population. In these circumstances, social networks were 'largely defensive or coping' in nature, and were characterised by 'amoral familism and clientelism' rather than a more generalised reciprocity; on the contrary, generalised trust was very low (Kolankiewicz 1996: 438). In moving from the bureaucratic administration of communism to the turbulent distribution mechanisms of market capitalism, what is remarkable is that Kolankiewicz detects considerable continuity in the role of social capital in Polish and Hungarian society. In particular, trust 'provides the element of predictability' that is undermined by the instability of capitalism, just as it was previously by the arbitrariness of bureaucracy (Kolankiewicz 1996: 437). Other studies have broadly confirmed the continuing importance of personal ties in post-communist societies, with some pointing to the persistence of ties among former communist administrators – the so-called *nomenklatura* – as a valuable business resource under capitalism (Clark 2000; Rose 1999; Ledeneva 1998). Sztompka similarly showed that family and intimate friendships were particularly important in post-communist Poland, particularly for those who were of low socio-economic status (Sztompka 1999: 130).

Socially valuable connections are, of course, less open to more marginal groups. The new urban poor in the post-communist countries are poor at least in part because their connections have little value in the new order. Alena Ledeneva gives the example of a traditional Russian folk saying: 'Do not have 100 roubles, do have 100 friends'; in the 1990s, the saying was reversed (Ledeneva 1998: 104, 175). In a telling comparison of social ties in Russia and Finland, Misztal has shown that Russians are far more likely than Finns to exchange goods and services through personal networks, and were also more likely to make use of relationships forged in the workplace;

but these ties were too clan-like to promote long-term dynamism or stimulate democratisation, and instead helped to form a 'second economy' that took place outside the public sphere (Misztal 2000: 224–5). This then extends the resources available for what in another context would unambiguously be viewed as perverse social capital, so that even the most peripheral are able to identify and exploit connections in developing alternative strategies for survival. In one study of street children in Moscow, it is said that,

> Young people use and accumulate specific social capital – previous connections with relatives and neighbours who were in prisons, records of joint criminal activities with their peers and older criminals, investment into the future links with adult criminals, and appropriation of the 'right notions' – in order to obtain the reputation and connections which are necessary for them to be accepted by the adult criminal community.
>
> (Stephenson 2001: 543)

Similarly, the post-Soviet Mafia in Russia arose largely among those who had no ties with the old *nomenklatura*, and drew instead on their own solidarity and codes of brotherhood (Ledeneva 1998: 190–1). In adjusting to the new forms of capitalism (which, in countries like Russia remain largely at odds with the inherited legal framework), the marginal need to invest in their networks in order to develop coping strategies. More affluent citizens can disinvest in social capital, and buy influence instead (Busse 2001).

In these circumstances, it is not surprising if social capital is less likely to produce benign consequences than in more stable conditions. There is accordingly little evidence in the post-communist nations that social networks and civic engagement are connected to democratisation. In a multi-country study of responses to the World Values Survey, Dowley and Silver found very little connection between levels of social capital and aggregate confidence in or satisfaction with democratic institutions (Dowley and Silver 2002). Although they consider a number of explanations for this lack of a connection between social capital and democratisation, they do not look at the most obvious one – namely, that those who are most engaged are better informed about politics, and are likely to be less than impressed with the people who now run things in the post-communist democracies. It is also possible that the affluent simply purchase decisions from policy-makers, rather than wasting time on the political process (Busse 2001). And although there is some evidence of an increase in voluntary organisations in the post-communist nations, much of this is apparently attributable to ethnic polarisation, with people joining groups that aggressively promote the interests of their own ethnic or national grouping (Dowley and Silver 2002: 511).

Of course, there are enormous differences between the experiences of, say, Poland, where real communists were always scarce, and a one-time communist superpower like Russia. Even before 1989, everyday life in the so-called Eastern block was always more varied and diverse than appeared in official portrayals. The available evidence suggests that particularised trust and bonding social capital have been essential in enabling people to survive and cope during a remarkable period of transition, and that connections to and among the old *nomenklatura* have continued to be of value for some time after the changes of 1989. In the more fragmented and dysfunctional societies, such as Russia, trading in a way that combines free market capitalism and observance of the law remains impossible, and many state officials are corrupt, so that the resources available for those whose strategies encompass unlawful activities are remarkably broad.

FAMILY AND INTIMATE TIES

For Coleman in particular, social capital was particularly expressed through primordial ties such as kinship. He particularly suggested that the origins of the most effective forms of social capital lay 'in the relationships established by childbirth' (Coleman 1991: 1–3). Coleman accordingly believed that social capital was weakened by processes that disrupted kinship ties, such as divorce and separation, or migration. As families left behind their existing networks of relatives, friends and other contacts, so the value of their social capital fell. Putnam has also noted that in general, 'emigration devalues one's social capital, for most of one's social connections must be left behind' (Putnam 2000: 390). Unlike Coleman, though, Putnam believes that the decline of the traditional family has had little impact on levels of civic engagement (Putnam 2000: 278–9).

Geographic mobility certainly appears to change the *sources* of social capital. This, incidentally, is an area where the Internet has started to make an early impact: in early 2002, some eight million British adults were said to be tracing old schoolmates through the website Friends Reunited (*The Times*, 3 January 2002). At a more specific level, the decision to move home within one's own community is well known to be a stressful one, which is not helped because it can strain people's sources of support. Americans who move home appear to turn more to friends in times of trouble, while the relatively immobile are more likely to call on family members (Boisjoly *et al*. 1995: 623). Among secondary school pupils in Toronto, family moves reportedly lead to earlier school leaving ages, but the loss of community resources can be offset by the level of family support available, with some fathers participating more fully in family life after a move, and some mothers offering higher levels of direct support to their children (Hagan *et al*. 1996: 381). While movement does cut off some ties, it also frees up time and energy among family members, which may in turn strengthen the immediate support that they can expect from one another. This is particularly apparent when we consider such eminently mobile groups as immigrants and refugees.

The importance of networks to migration decisions is well known. The term 'chain migration', for instance, has long been used to describe the tendency of new migrants to seek places where they have friends or kin, who then provide a resource to facilitate adjustment and also possibly help compensate for the lack of other resources such as cash or qualifications (Brettell 2000). This has been repeatedly demonstrated both from studies of host communities and supplier communities. Strong evidence is available for the role of family connections in chain migration, for example among Mexicans migrating to the USA and elsewhere, even after controlling for other variables such as the possession of human capital (Palloni *et al*. 2001). Similarly with refugees. One particularly valuable study has drawn on long-term follow-up studies of refugees escaping persecution after the collapse of the Ottoman empire in the early twentieth century. From observation and interviews conducted over some decades in Cyprus, Peter Loizos argues that not only did people re-establish old social linkages, but also used prior links to form new relationships 'in which a modicum of trust was extended simply because a person was linked to a known community' (Loizos 2000: 130). After settling and then recovering from the short-term crises of settlement, Loizos observed that while some families preferred to marry within their own group, other families developed strategies of selective intermarriage (arranged by parents) with the host community, which in turn required considerable reputational knowledge on the part of both families, so that individuals and families became 'structurally and intimately linked by consanguinity and affinity', offering a greatly enhanced capacity for cooperative action (Loizos 2000: 137).

Nor has the family collapsed. On the contrary, it appears to be remarkably durable. A survey for the *Observer* newspaper in Britain found that the most trusted figures among 11–21-year-olds were parents, with 72 per cent reporting that they trusted them 'a lot', and only 3 per cent saying they did not trust them (Summerskill 2002). However, there is some evidence that peer groups are catching up: friends came close behind parents in the list of most trusted people, and although parents were more frequently cited than friends as most trusted source of information about 'sex and growing up' (31 per cent against 22 per cent), in practice the position was dramatically reversed, with far more young people saying they had learned most from friends than parents (27 per cent as against 7 per cent). Yet certainly there is some evidence of a decline in family-based social capital in Europe as in the USA. The authors of a study of juvenile delinquency and right-wing extremism in Berlin found that parental monitoring seemed much less important as a protective factor than they had expected. Rather, the key risk factors appeared to be membership of a peer group that preferred antisocial leisure activities, and a sense of anomie arising from (perceived) vulnerability to the repeated economic and political crises that have affected the life chances of young Berliners (Boehnke *et al.* 2000). Finally, the separation of couples almost invariably is associated with a reduction in levels of trust (Hall 1999: 444).

Yet if family is relatively less important as a source of close ties, friendship appears to be growing. In a major study of friendship, Ray Pahl and Liz Spencer have analysed data from cohort studies such as the British Household Panel Study, which allow for longitudinal study of changes over time, and conclude that they show increasing evidence of 'the growth of friendship and friend-like relationships'. Friend-like behaviour, they argue, is also increasingly typical of kinship relations, in that 'they are voluntarily chosen; they are developed not given; and they help to strengthen our own distinctive individuality' (Pahl and Spencer 1997: 102–3). One German author has spoken of a 'verticalisation' of family structures, combined with a shift in behaviour from family as a fixed institution towards family as a network – or, perhaps, even a network of networks (Neyer 1995: 233–4). Moreover, unconditional trust in a loved one is not intrinsically a positive phenomenon; it may rather represent reliance on habit and authority, so that some degree of mistrust within intimate relationships is arguably rational, and possibly desirable. So where family ties remain, they may be changing in nature, at least to some extent.

Common sense suggests that less importance attaches to family ties, at least of the traditional kind, as a result of increased mobility and growing levels of marital breakdown. But this is a somewhat narrow and short-term view of the changes going on in intimate relationships. In the longer run, it looks as though the stereotypical nuclear family of the mid-twentieth century was a short-lived and exceptional arrangement; couple arrangements in earlier times were not as durable as they are in the early twenty-first century, not least because one of the partners was far more likely to die at a relatively young age (often the woman, in or after childbirth). But what is probably more significant is the very broad range of changes that are taking place in intimate relationships (Jamieson 1998). Today, the lengthening of the lifespan means that in Europe, America and much of Asia, families frequently span four generations and might even span five. Yet while these intergenerational linkages are expanding, the number of children has shrunk steadily, so many children grow up on their own, or only have stepbrothers and stepsisters, and growing numbers of women decide not to have children at all. Child-rearing is still rare among same-sex partnerships, though it may grow as a result of recent changes in the law. If we combine this with the increasingly elective nature of intimate ties in general, then it is possible to discern the basis for a qualitative change in people's social capital as a result of changes in the family. This is far from saying that family has collapsed, or that the demise of the traditional family has necessarily depleted people's stocks of social capital. Rather, changes in intimate relationships are consistent with increased reliance on friendship and other ties, and are also possibly producing a convergence between family and other types of linkage. If so, this has significant consequences for our theory of social capital, as it further undermines the clear boundaries between bridging and bonding ties.

SOCIAL CAPITAL IN RISK SOCIETY: FLEXIBLE FRIENDS?

Fixed coordinates, in social life as in road maps, provide security and stability. Yet formal organisations are rule bound, and cannot have the flexibility and sensitivity of informal networks (Rose 1999: 150). They are unable to adjust to rapid changes in their environment, nor to sharp internal shocks, ranging from embezzlement by a senior partner to infidelity by a loved one. In conditions dominated by a shift towards flexibility and the general breakdown of hierarchy and authority, fixed coordinates in social life are ever less relevant. Working relationships, so long the nest in which male identities were nurtured, are increasingly characterised by adaptability, mobility and the capacity to teamwork with new colleagues as smoothly as one discards old ones (Employment Department 1996). The student revolts of the 1960s, and the wider spread of post-materialist values among the young, have reduced the deference of the general population (Hall 1999: 446). For Peter Senge, prophet of the learning organisation, self-organisation is incompatible with top-down planning and bureaucratic regulation; rather, it can be managed and led only through self-regulation (Senge 1990: 387).

So there appears to be a tendency for social arrangements to become more provisional, perhaps more experimental. For Richard Sennett, among others, these are risky trends, which threaten to unravel the very fabric of individual character (Sennett 1999). Does this spell death for social capital? Or does it imply new roles for networks, in the absence of other mechanisms for coordinating social behaviour?

On balance, it seems that postmodern conditions are more favourable than inauspicious for social capital. Empirically, this chapter has provided evidence from a number of countries of growth in small-scale and informal forms of civic engagement, such as the rise of self-help groups. These groups appeal to people not simply for instrumental reasons, but because they open up opportunities for self-determination (including the prospects of challenging expert wisdom), and allow people a measure of control over their commitment. They also offer access to connections that are 'identity-relevant' (Heinze and Strünck 2000: 202), in that all members can participate on the basis of common experiences of a particular issue or problem. More generally, communities of interest that focus on a distinctive lifestyle frequently offer access to a wide variety of networks: gay and lesbian people who move from one town to another will often find it relatively easy to gain access to networks based on shared sexual preferences, despite the fact that as newcomers they do not already know anyone (Hill 1996).

More theoretically, Piotr Sztompka has argued that the social significance of trust has increased as a result of increasing international interdependency, the complexities of an extreme division of labour, the growth of manufactured risk, and the constant presence of strangers through travel and migration (Sztompka 1999: 11–14). In the field of business transactions, Fukuyama plausibly argues that trust plays a more significant role as economic activity becomes more complex and more technologically sophisticated; even the much-heralded efficiency gains to be obtained from flat hierarchies depend entirely on workers' social capital (Fukuyama 2001: 10). The influential American economist Michael Porter, for example, has argued that while globalisation is reducing the importance of some old reasons for clusters of firms to congregate in a particular local area, such as ease of access to raw materials, firms can also benefit from clusters in the new economy, for example in terms of gaining access to knowledge and expertise (Porter 2000). In short, people's ability to access resources through their connections is certainly not diminishing in importance. If the past fifty years are characterised by the constancy of change, it seems that their overall effect on social capital has been to increase rather than diminish its significance. If overall levels of social capital were truly in decline, then, the consequences would be serious.

The evidence presented in this chapter does not appear to reflect a general tendency of decline in levels of social capital. Rather, it broadly confirms that the individualisation of social relations, and the pervasive refashioning of identity, are changing the nature and meaning of people's relationships. Of course, for rational choice theorists this would come as no surprise. Viewing human behaviour as the outcome of individuals' decisions as to which investments are optimal for their purposes, rational choice theorists believe that social capital is thus the product of a series of individual decisions (Glaeser *et al*. 2002). But this seems a rather ahistorical view, which ignores the varying circumstances in which individuals make their choices. The Beck–Giddens thesis seems rather better suited to explain how and why social capital appears to be changing. As Kirchhöfer has written in respect of individuals, with a strong sense of irony,

> Social networks are increasing in significance for the individualised social shaping of the individual. Visible and tangible social networks are coming to replace traditional collective structures, which are being eroded. . . . Small structures offer a subjective social structure of relevance, they are a space of choice and source of resources.
>
> (Kirchhöfer 2000: 15; see also Raffo and Reeves 2000)

In a world that is bent on living beyond its resources, ecologically and economically if not psychologically, Beck heralds the arrival of what he calls 'a co-operative or altruistic individualism' which embraces the defence of life as a personal project and rejects subordination to the demands of an untrammeled market system, on the one hand, and a communitarianism that imposes purity and homogeneity, on the other (Beck 2000: 171–2). From this perspective, then, the move towards more open, fluid and temporary forms of social capital appears to be part of a much wider process of social and cultural change.

5

SOCIAL CAPITAL AS POLICY

Most scholarly thinking makes little if any impact in the wider world. Countless notions come to be formulated, systematised, debated, applied, criticised and evaluated, before vanishing into the dusty archives of the history of ideas. Social capital is not like that. Its sudden rise to prominence in the social sciences has touched a wider public. Thanks to the lively populist streak in his language, Putnam has gifted headline writers a series of vivid and easy attention-grabbers, such as television being a 'culprit', or proliferations of picnics and choirs as a solution. The interdisciplinary character of the concept has created wide coalitions of scholars with differing academic expertise, and of course they have also focussed on issues that engage policy-makers, such as health, crime, regeneration, employment and educational attainment. Treating networks and shared norms as a form of capital has given the idea some resonance among economists, opening doors into the usually closed, clubby world of serious policy debate. And the language of capital has immediate practical purchase among a wider audience: after all, if you can have capital, you can invest prudently in it, or you can hide it under the bed and let its value dwindle.

This chapter explores the growing debate over social capital as a policy tool. The fact that social capital has consequences independent of other structural factors means that, in principle, the insights of the social capital debate should be amenable to application. Moreover, the concept has been taken up by a number of influential policy-making bodies. It has been promoted with the Organisation for Economic Co-operation and Development, a body which serves as a forum for policy discussion between the governments of the world's most affluent nations (including not only the usual suspects, such as Britain, France, Germany and the USA, but also relative newcomers like Mexico and South Korea). The policy implications of social capital have also been developed within the World Bank, mainly in the context of a series of consultative workshops held through the mid-1990s when the Bank was formulating policies on sustainable development. These ideas were subsequently implemented in the Bank's poverty reduction programmes, which emphasised community-driven development, community group participation in decision-making, building local organisational capacity, and selecting projects that meet local demand (Narayan and Pritchett 1999: 284–90).

The idea and language of social capital has come to provide a broad common platform for dialogue between policy-makers and academics. Robert Putnam's willingness to engage in policy discussion is particularly well known. In an article published in the same year as his major study of Italian government, Putnam called for 'wise public policies to revitalise America's stocks of social capital' (Putnam 1993b: 18), and he has vigorously pursued opportunities to engage with the policy community ever since. He devoted the final chapter of *Bowling Alone* to defining an 'agenda for social capitalists'. Admittedly, this was brief in length: twelve pages, two of which are given over to general reflection on the task of rebuilding community in America. Putnam concluded that deciding how to create social capital was 'no simple task'; while it might be 'eased by a palpable national crisis, like war or natural disaster . . . America at the dawn of the new century faces no such galvanising crisis' (Putnam 2000: 402). A year after *Bowling Alone* appeared in the bookshops, Putnam's proposition was put brutally to the test. As well as commenting publicly on the short-term impact of the 11 September attacks on social solidarity, Putnam was consulted extensively by the White House; as well as going out of his way to be seen visiting a mosque, President Bush used his subsequent State of the Union Address to announce the creation of a citizen corps and urge Americans to do 'something good' for one another. Putnam himself, it should be added, found these gestures encouraging but insufficient (Putnam 2002).

There have also been echoes of interest among Third Way thinkers in Europe. In Britain, New Labour's policy interest in social capital predates its 1997 election victory; the concept played a part in the thinking of the Commission for Social Justice, which was charged by the Labour Party leadership in opposition with reviewing its whole approach to social policy (Commission for Social Justice 1994: 308). One New Labour thinker has argued that the creation of social capital can help answer 'what is probably the most pressing question our society faces', namely how to build solidarity in a secular society exposed to the full rigours of a global market and committed to the principle of individual choice (Leadbeater 1997: 35). Another New Labour author, introducing an article by Tony Blair, described social capital as bringing a 'tougher edge' to traditional left-wing thought on community, fellowship or fraternity (Thompson 2002: 1). Blair did not mention social capital in his article, which talked about community, but he has mentioned the term briefly and positively elsewhere (Blair 2001: 13). Putnam's influence on the Bush administration was noted with interest by one of Blair's think tanks (Performance and Innovation Unit 2002: 50), and the Office for National Statistics embarked in 2001 on a research project designed to inform government policy and encourage the collection of official statistical data on social capital (Harper 2001: 26). Even centrist Conservatives have got in on the act, with a fringe meeting at their party conference organised by the environmentalist charity Groundwork on the topic of 'The moral market: why Conservatives believe in social capital' (Groundwork 2002). In general, then, if somewhat cautiously when it comes to concrete measures, centrist and left-centrist policy-makers have expressed considerable interest in social capital's policy potential.

Government interest, so far, has often concentrated more on measuring and monitoring social capital than doing much about it. This chapter starts by considering why social capital should become a focus of policy, particularly given the high risks of intervention producing the opposite results from those intended. It then explores the question of measurement, and asks why it has become such a concern for the policy community. Next, the chapter examines a number of attempts to operationalise the idea of social capital for policy purposes. Finally, it considers the prospects for policy in what remains a complex, contradictory and uncertain area. In these circumstances, the future of social capital as a tool and goal of policy inevitably remains open.

WHY DEVELOP POLICIES FOR SOCIAL CAPITAL?

As we have already seen, Putnam has certainly not been shy about the policy potential of his ideas. Even in the early 1990s, he argued that the Clinton administration's job-training programmes for the unemployed would work far better if complemented by the creation of new linkages between community groups, schools, employers and workers (Putnam 1993b: 5). *Bowling Alone* contains an entire chapter full of proposals, though it is of course consistent with Putnam's thinking that most of these are addressed more to his readers and the wider community than to policy-makers (Putnam 2000: 402–14). Coleman was slightly more ambivalent about the potential for political intervention. He certainly accepted that there were risks of market failure in the production of social capital as a by-product of activities undertaken for other purposes, and thought it likely that social capital as a public good would suffer from under-investment (Coleman 1994: 312–13). However, he also suspected that state intervention might make matters worse rather than better, not least because the essence of social capital is that it consists of activities and relationships freely engaged in by individuals, which could only suffer if government stepped in and replaced them.

Some people do not think there should be any intervention to build social capital. Some writers within a neo-Marxist tradition have claimed that the concept has been deliberately used to distract attention from the underlying materialist and structural causes of inequality (Muntaner *et al.* 2000; McClenaghan 2000). Certainly some forms of Third Way thinking have presented social capital more or less explicitly as an alternative to social democratic welfare policies. For Charles Leadbeater, for instance, investment in social capital is desirable because of its dividend: 'a stronger community, more able to look after itself, with stronger bonds of trust and co-operation' (Leadbeater 1997: 34). Mai Wann similarly proposes a strategy of 'building social capital' in order to create a welfare system based on the principle of subsidiarity, through active public support for self-help and mutual aid groups (Wann 1995). So the idea that social capital is a fig-leaf for welfare cuts is not entirely groundless. For Mitchell Dean, who draws on both Foucault and critical theory, Putnam differs little from Margaret Thatcher; measures to promote engagement are 'technologies of citizenship' that are the more subtle because they draw on 'individuals' exercise of freedom and self-responsibility' (Dean 1999: 152–68). For Avis and others, the use of the term 'capital' is sufficient to give the game away: it is to accept that the limits to debate are set within the parameters of capitalist relations, downplaying the conflicts of interest that characterise these relations (Avis 2002; Blaxter and Hughes 2001). Maxine Molyneux is highly critical of the gendered assumptions that she detects behind the new development agenda, and believes that the women's rights agenda is likely to be incompatible with policies based around social capital (Molyneux 2002).

It has also been suggested that social capital is related to communitarianism, with its romanticised view of local bonds and tradition-based solidarity (Muntaner *et al.* 2000; Raffo and Reeves 2000; Morrow 1999: 748). Particularly as formulated by Coleman, the concept seems highly congruent with communitarianism, with its emphasis on the 'parenting deficit' (Etzioni 1993) as the source of many of the ills of modern society. Undoubtedly, the high rate of divorce and separation in Western societies has changed the context in which children acquire a sense of their own place in the wider world; it is quite conceivable (though as yet unproven) that this has had some effect on overall levels of social trust in the West. Nor can there be much argument that stability and security are needed in childhood; family breakdowns can be catastrophic for children's sense of self-esteem. Yet the non-nuclear family can also provide access to a wider range of sources of social support, and also enhance confidence and build social skills. Further, as Misztal points out, although stepfamilies have a higher rate of collapse during the first two years, thereafter they tend to outlive more conventional relationships (Misztal 1996: 169). The jury is still out on the impact of family breakdown on social capital in the West.

Equally sceptical views have been expressed by writers from a neo-liberal perspective. Thus Fukuyama warns that some activities are best left to civil society: excessive state intervention 'can have a serious negative impact on social capital' (Fukuyama 2001: 18). Government intervention in an area like civic engagement could even be seen as an intrusion on the individual's freedom. However, he concedes that it is possible that governments may well decide to attack some forms of social capital. Examples of this might include state action to stamp out behaviour leading to economic inefficiency, such as cronyism and cartels in the business world, or the use of networks to favour the careers of a particular privileged ethnic group or gender. In such cases, a considerable body of public opinion would support policy action against the negative effects of social capital. Otherwise, he believes that matters are generally best left to the initiative of individuals. Frank Furedi has suggested that policies designed to promote volunteering inevitably end up by degrading the meaning of volunteering, as the existence of inducements removes the element of altruism and channels people into doing something more out of self-interest than from a desire to serve others (Furedi 2002: 24–5).

The prospects of unintended consequences – including negative or perverse results – seem high. Of course, this may be true for many policy areas, but the promotion of social capital is particularly fraught with difficulties. Some of these arise from the fact that the promotion of social capital depends on other actors than the state's own agents; it can only be built by engaging civic society. This means that policy must act at a distance, working through partners and intermediaries who may then act in unanticipated ways. For example, a policy aimed at promoting volunteering by providing funds to voluntary bodies may end up by encouraging competition rather than cooperation among those who are applying for funds, and displacing civic activists with paid professionals. Policies designed to mobilise voluntary bodies as service delivery agents may inadvertently suppress their capacity to nurture social capital (Lowndes and Wilson 2001: 641). Or, as Antar Dhesi has pointed out, in contexts where formal institutions may be in conflict with informal institutions, policy interventions may impose undesirable constraints upon collective action, and thereby inhibit the development of social capital (Dhesi 2000).

Nor is there much evidence of enthusiasm for the concept among professionals and others involved in the fields that are being addressed. Harry Salmon, an experienced British community activist and Methodist minister, suggests that many of those working in community development are 'wary' of the term (Salmon 2002: 49). Similar reservations were expressed by community-based workers in Northern Ireland (Morrissey and McGinn 2001: 17). Nor would the term have appealed to an earlier generation of Marxist-influenced radicals in community development. Even those who favour firm government action acknowledge that some aspects of social capital are probably beyond reach, not least because of the importance of historical and cultural factors in its creation (Performance and Innovation Unit 2002: 53).

So even those who believe that policy is required often emphasise the complexity involved. In his original study of political institutions in Italy, Putnam emphasised the path-dependent nature of social capital. In other words, he presented the distribution of social capital in contemporary Italy as being the outcome of long-standing processes with their roots in the distant past (Putnam 1993a). If the Norman invasion of Sicily and southern Italy is to blame for the weakness of its civil society today, then it follows that short-term political intervention is most unlikely to take instant effect (Lemann 1996: 24). Ralf Dahrendorf, in considering the challenges of building an effective civil society in Central and Eastern Europe, thought that a minimum of two generations would be required. He warned that too deliberate and planned an approach was

> all too likely to produce a Brasilia rather than a Rio de Janeiro, an artificial construct which people yearn to escape for the nooks and crannies of the real thing.
>
> (Dahrendorf 1990: 96)

Others have recognised that although the impacts of institution-building policies can be lasting and sustainable, it 'may take several generations' before they are felt (Maskell and Törnqvist 1999: 77–9; see also Young 2002). This is simply too long a timescale for most politicians in a democratic society.

The case for policy intervention in the creation of social capital is a broad one. First, and most direct, is the fact that people's ability to access resources through their social capital can make a considerable difference to their life chances. In so far as the state is expected to intervene in the distribution of resources more generally, in areas such as health or education, social capital represents a tool of policy. In so far as social capital can itself be seen as a public good, it represents a goal of policy. Policies which promote social capital can therefore directly influence the well-being of the wider community. For some, the attraction of social capital as a policy concept lies in its potential as an alternative to human capital theory. Paul Thompson, for example, has described human capital theory as excessively individualistic, whereas social capital 'focusses on the connectedness of resources, and therefore on issues of differential access, power and inequality' (Thompson 2002: 4). For others, by contrast, social capital provides an accompaniment to human capital, complementing rather than displacing its insights into the economics of education and training (OECD 2001a, 2001b; World Bank 2001). Rather different approaches flow from these two views, but both are agreed on the need to devise policies designed to promote the creation of social capital.

Second, policy decisions already have an impact on social capital. One official report listed seven existing sets of policies and programmes that it saw as contributing to the accumulation of beneficial social capital in the UK, including support for the voluntary sector, the promotion of business sector clusters, and citizenship education in schools (Performance and Innovation Unit 2002: 57–8). Sometimes, though, policy decisions have the unintended side effect of eroding social capital, or even of creating perverse social capital. In the case of British post-war housing policy, for example, what policy-makers wanted to do was clear slums and replace them rapidly with cost effective, healthy and attractive modern housing. It is widely agreed that, whatever the merits of this policy in its own right, it had the unintended consequence of destroying many existing neighbourly connections in working-class areas and creating inward-looking enclaves with low aspirations (Performance and Innovation Unit 2002: 54). In similar vein, Perri 6 argues that most government job-training schemes tend to reinforce 'the wrong kind of networks . . . where they only meet other unemployed people much like themselves' (6 1997: 6). It has also been claimed that privatisation damages social capital by shifting responsibility for providing services to private individuals or groups, who may favour very narrow, particularistic forms of cooperation (Champlin 1999). Drawing on an empirical study of friendship ties in Britain, Pahl and Spencer have criticised community development strategies based on 'old style ties based on gender, race or ethnicity as a way of empowering disadvantaged categories' on the ground that these 'may, unwittingly, have added to their troubles by making it more difficult for such close-knit groups to develop bridging ties' (Pahl and Spencer 1997: 102). Moreover, in developing measures to promote social capital, of course, policy-makers are not starting with a blank sheet.

Third, other actors in society recognise the importance of social capital. If public policy ignores their actions, and the consequences which flow from them, then these actors may use social capital in ways which are undesirable. For example, Ledeneva notes that while many Western companies in Russia see *blat* as undesirable, others have decided to go with the flow; as an illustration, she cites Nestlé's policy of using *blat* to recruit reliable workers (Ledeneva 1998: 207). Yet while recruitment through connections can be a highly reliable way of attracting amployees, it can also exclude not only the unreliable, but those who are simply outsiders with no existing contacts on the inside. And indeed much public policy is explicitly designed to prevent people from using their connections inappropriately. In the UK, for example, politicians and senior public servants are required to declare any membership of the Freemasons.

Fourth, the idea of social capital may help to shift government away from what is often seen as a deficit model of disadvantage. Much of the dominant literature on topics such as economic growth, health promotion, educational equality, regeneration and community development tends to imply that it is the disadvantaged who are somehow lacking – in education, in skills, in the 'right' attitudes – and who therefore need to be transformed.

The idea of social capital, by contrast, emphasises resources that communities already have, and therefore allows attention to turn to the ways in which external agencies work and interact with them (Hibbitt *et al.* 2001: 159; Woolcock 2001: 15). It is highly congruent with the emerging interest in partnership as a basis for policy development, and therefore can provide a basis for ensuring that the least advantaged are not excluded from strategic partnerships.

Finally, there is also evidence that many citizens are concerned about the erosion of social capital. In Colombia and Guatemala, researchers reported frequent complaints from the urban poor about the lack of social fabric and the resulting climate of fear (McIlwaine and Moser 2001: 971). Concern about community appears to be more widespread among disadvantaged groups than among the privileged, presumably because the latter are able to use other resources to protect their interests. Yet their decisions in turn may (largely unintentionally) damage the social capital of the wider society. If the affluent build walls and hire armed guards to protect themselves against crime, for example, the poor are further ghettoised into zones of multiple vulnerability.

There are, then, practical reasons for suggesting that social capital might serve as the focus for policy development. This is not to deny the difficulties that are inherent in developing such policies in practice. Repeatedly, this book has emphasised that social capital is a multifaceted and complex concept which refers to relationships rather than to things. This makes it particularly slippery as a focus for policy. Of course, it is not alone in this: security, justice, freedom from oppression, human rights and even lifelong learning are all equally elusive concepts which defy simplistic treatment. This does not mean that policy-makers can be allowed to ignore them. Yet while the practical basis for policy development is clear, the philosophical basis is less clear-cut. Those who embrace a neo-Marxist view of the world, or espouse a neo-liberal perspective on the economy, are unlikely to change their minds when it comes to social capital. Their projects lie elsewhere.

MEASURING SOCIAL CAPITAL

Policy-makers who embrace the idea of promoting social capital are virtually unanimous in agreeing that measurement is a central challenge (OECD 2001a: 4; OECD 2001b: 39; Harper 2001). The Forward Studies Unit report in Britain, for example, has argued that 'it is crucial' to be able to measure social capital at all levels and in all its forms and types, and then relate these to particular economic, social and other outcomes of concern to policy-makers (Performance and Innovation Unit 2002: 52). A wide range of bodies involved in community development has accepted that measuring social capital can be an effective way of influencing funders and policy-makers (Walker *et al.* 2000). Contemporary policy-makers generally choose to invest scarce resources in activities that can be measured, so that the results of their investment can be compared with the outcomes of similar outlays elsewhere. Social capital is certainly no exception to this rule.

For some, particularly in the business community, measurement of social capital is simply a matter of examining 'the bottom line' (Prusack and Cohen 2001: 87). But this is not as easy as it looks. As the OECD bluntly puts it, 'Measurement of social capital is difficult' (OECD 2001b: 43). Much existing work has been based on measures that were exported wholesale from the USA, with minimal adaptation (Harper 2001: 12). Yet relationships and shared values are deeply rooted in local circumstances, and people experience the effects in very different ways. As the OECD points out, 'Much of what is relevant to social capital is tacit and relational, defying easy measurement or classification' (OECD 2001b: 43). In these circumstances, any indicators inevitably are proxies, which do not measure social capital directly. Proxies are basically 'easy variables'; they must have some clear connection to social capital, and they must be easy to measure (or even are already being measured). At best, the fit will be very loose indeed, and at worst it may be so baggy as to mislead rather than inform.

One resulting difficulty is the sheer range of potential indicators, all of which point to different dimensions. In *Bowling Alone*, Putnam devised a composite index of fourteen separate measures of formal and informal associational activities and levels of trust (Putnam 2000). One template, developed for Northern Ireland according to the policy priorities identified by the devolved government at four different levels from individual to civic, proposed nineteen separate indicators (Morrissey and McGinn 2001: 70–2). An analysis in 2001 of the main large-scale surveys in the UK identified eighteen which had already developed a significant social capital element, including the British Crime Survey, the British Household Panel Survey and the UK Time Use Survey (Harper 2001: 18–19). Tom Schuller has emphasised the dangers of 'bundling up' indicators of social capital that measure the attributes of a range of levels of social unit, from the individual to the family to the neighbourhood to the organisation to the nation, when social capital depends critically on its embeddedness in a particular context

(Schuller 2000; see also Whitehead and Diederichsen 2001). One British government adviser has reached a similar conclusion, calling for a simple 'quick and dirty' indicator that politicians can readily understand and apply (Harper 2001: 14). Yet the selection of a limited set of indicators is also highly risky.

The OECD believes that 'trust may be an acceptable proxy . . . in the absence of a wider and more comprehensive set of indicators' (OECD 2001b: 45). At one level, the measurement of trust is straightforward. Since 1981, the World Values Survey (WVS), led by Ron Inglehart, has asked a number of questions on trust, including the following (World Values Survey 2000):

Generally speaking, would you say that most people can be trusted, or that you need to be very careful in dealing with people?

Responses are then divided into three categories:

- Most people can be trusted
- Need to be very careful
- Don't know

In 1995–6, the OECD country with the highest levels of trust on this measure was Norway (65.3 per cent) and the lowest was Turkey (6.5 per cent), with the UK coming in between (31 per cent) (OECD 2001b: 44). But the apparent simplicity of this measure can be extremely misleading. Translating the question into different languages raises enormous questions over the meaning of the results; to take one very simple example, the German word *Vertrauen* means both trust and confidence, but the English version of the WVS asks questions on both subjects. Even within a single language community, definitions of trust can vary, as can the overtones that people associate with the word itself. This is certainly not to decry the use of quantitative data, including the findings from the WVS, but rather to accept that the measurement of trust remains a 'great lacuna' in research into the impact of social capital (Glaeser *et al.* 2000: 811). However, as we have seen, trust is not in itself a dimension of social capital but an outcome, so this can only be a partial solution which might be suitable for some purposes at some times. It cannot provide a general all-purpose indicator. But then what can?

Repeatedly throughout this book, we have seen that there are several different types of social capital. It is not always benign, it is not always unidirectional, and it does not always appear in uniform units. Bourdieu's concept of social capital perhaps particularly exemplifies the problems, as he uses the metaphor of capital with deliberate precision. But whereas economic capital is almost always convertible, there is absolutely no guarantee that the different types of social capital can be valued in units of a single currency. As Warde and Tampubolon put it, 'it might be better conceived in terms of different currencies, implying that on some occasions converting dollars into roubles or euros will be difficult' (Warde and Tampubolon 2002: 175). Or, more pragmatically still, policy-makers may be forced to accept that some indicators will do for some purposes, and some for others.

OPERATIONALISING POLICIES FOR SOCIAL CAPITAL

Britain provides an interesting example of growing interest among policy-makers in identifying the implications of social capital. After the UK publication of *Bowling Alone*, Putnam led a group of policy advisers, which included the social capital scholar David Halpern, in a seminar at Number 10 Downing Street. Halpern, by then a senior policy adviser in the Forward Strategies Unit in the Cabinet Office, had previously been an academic and had published a number of highly regarded studies of social capital (Halpern 2001). One thinker associated with New Labour has suggested that 'the politics of social capital lend themselves to progressive public policy with a central role for the state as a capacity builder' (Thompson 2002: 4). DEMOS, a leading New Labour think tank, has examined social capital in relation to urban regeneration, calling for the promotion of 'social entre-preneurs' to create partnerships in disadvantaged communities, and help overcome the effects of what might be called network poverty within those communities (Leadbeater 1997: 34). Perri 6, then DEMOS' director of policy and research, who has been widely credited with promoting the notion of network poverty as a cause of social exclusion, argued in the late 1990s that government should be concerned with 'enabling people to develop and use their networks' (6 1997: 6). There has, then, been no shortage of debate over social capital within the New Labour policy community.

Generally, though, these signs of policy interest in Britain have rarely been translated into action. Nor is it easy to spell out precisely how governments should act to promote social capital. As Fukuyama has observed, it is one thing for public policy-makers to be aware of the existing sources of social capital and alert to its positive benefits, and quite another to be able to point to obvious levers that can be pulled in order to create it (Fukuyama 2001: 17). And if they do develop concrete policy measures, it is also hard to quantify and monitor the outcomes.

Nevertheless, there have been some clear signals from policy-makers, and in particular from international bodies such as the World Bank and OECD. The World Bank's adoption of the concept has had particularly far-reaching consequences; on the one hand, the concept has provided key individuals within the Bank with a way of broadening the debate about measuring the returns on its investments in sustainable development; on the other, it has led the Bank to develop policies for social and cultural change alongside its existing measures for economic adjustment (Grootaert 1996; Serageldin and Grootaert 1999). The conceptual debate within the World Bank was paralleled by vigorous lobbying efforts by some national governments and non-governmental organisations in favour of a more 'participatory' and 'bottom-up' approach to development, which would 'build capacity' by supporting existing poor people's organisations, in ways that were sensitive to the institutional context in which these organisations operate (Fox 1997: 964–5).

British policy-makers also shifted in 2002 from a broad if noncommittal interest to a more clearly specified attempt at policy formulation. In April 2002, the Forward Strategy Unit (FSU) produced a discussion paper on social capital which sought to identify a firm basis for policy development. The rationale for government intervention lay both in a general claim that social capital is vital 'in supporting and nurturing virtuous norms and behaviours such as co-operation with others', and in more specific arguments about its role in promoting economic efficiency, equity, and civic engagement (Performance and Innovation Unit 2002: 52). Although it started with a review of the benefits from social capital, the FSU balanced these with a recognition of its dark side, and also acknowledged that some of the benefits depended precisely on inequality of access to social capital (some of the value of networks in job search, for example, is lost if everyone knows everybody). The FSU concluded that policy should be directed towards building social capital as a public good rather than a club good, with a particular focus on creating bridging social capital so as to transcend social, ethnic, religious and other divides (Performance and Innovation Unit 2002: 33).

More precisely, several observers have concluded that there are indeed a number of levers that policy-makers may pull in order to promote social capital. Education offers a particularly direct means of investing in social capital. Fukuyama suggests that the most direct way for the state to generate social capital is through education, which helps people build social skills and engage in shared norms and rules (Fukuyama 2001: 18). Similarly, the OECD claims that 'education and learning can support habits, skills and values conducive to social co-operation and participation' (OECD 2001b: 13). Empirically, the connection between education and engagement is well established (Hall 1999: 435–7; Wilson 1997). As Erika Hayes James has pointed out in respect of Black managers in the USA, training is an opportunity both to increase individual human capital *and* to extend membership in professional networks (James 2000: 504). There is also a broader sense in which education and social capital are connected, in that cooperation and reciprocity are produced by processes of social learning (Wilson 1997). Glaeser emphasises the association of schooling with social capital, and speculates that this has arisen because successful experiences in school and college foster better social skills, not just through the academic element but also through informal and extra-curricular encounters such as those provided through sports and club (Glaeser 2001: 391). Yet much of the learning that is most relevant to the creation of social capital takes place outside formal educational institutions, and it is therefore difficult for policy-makers – governmental or corporate – to know how to influence it.

Distinguishing between policies at the individual or micro-level, the community or meso-level, and national or macro-level, the FSU recommended that the British Cabinet should consider a wide range of possible initiatives. At individual level, these included active promotion of parenting skills in schools and in the community, encouragement for mentoring programmes, the use of residential activities to help build new networks for young people involved in petty crime, and support for volunteering among young people and older adults. Community-level initiatives embraced proposals for extending Internet access in socially mixed areas, and new approaches to urban planning and design to make social interaction easier and create more socially mixed communities. At national level, FSU recommended community service credit schemes that allow members to exchange hours of time on services in kind, as well as the promotion of service learning in schools and universities, the use of citizens' juries as a means of engaging local communities in policy debate, and measures designed to counteract the decline in political activity among the young, such as children's parliaments. Broadly, then, much thought has already gone into the development of policies to support engagement and promote volunteering. The major challenge may well be to ensure that these reach all parts of the community, and particularly help bridge networks of access and influence across ethnic, racial and linguistic boundaries.

Government can clearly benefit from social capital. Since the 1980s, many governments in Europe have sought to create partnerships with voluntary organisations as a way of delivering core services. The advantages include the simple fact that the service users may trust the voluntary organisations, but be deeply sceptical of the state's own agencies. This is particularly important, as the most excluded individuals and groups tend to be the most distrustful when faced with plans for consultation and capacity-building (Bockmeyer 2000: 2417). Strategies built around social capital, whether or not they are explicitly named as such, can provide one mechanism for overcoming mistrust. For example, disabled people in Britain are profoundly (and very reasonably) suspicious of any vocational training scheme which might be used to place their benefits at risk. By involving voluntary organisations that are known and trusted, such as national charities like the Shaw Trust, the British government has been able to help significant numbers of disabled people to participate in its New Deal programme of training and job placement (Heenan 2002: 390–1). Of course, for such schemes to work over the longer term, they have to deliver in ways that meet the service users' needs, or the pattern of institutionalised distrust simply spreads to encompass the voluntary agencies as well. Policies based on social capital can therefore help improve the effectiveness of government, particularly in complex areas where many different arms of government have a potential interest in finding solutions.

Social capital has been widely used in development policy, partly as a result of the interest shown by the World Bank. But, as Katherine Rankin argues, its attractiveness lies in its capacity to mobilise local social networks in tackling the problems of poverty, as for example in the preference for locally rooted strategies such as microfinance programmes. Rankin has gone on to argue that what is required in such cases is a critically informed approach that could engage women's solidarity to challenge dominant gender ideologies (Rankin 2002; see also McIlwaine and Moser 2001).

Partnership-based approaches have been widely advocated as a way of promoting social capital. It has been suggested, for example, that involving communities actively in decision-making and programme implementation is a way of promoting sustainable changes in health, as well as tacking inequalities in health (Davies 2001). Local government, it is suggested, is of particular relevance here through its potential influence on the local 'political opportunity structure': that is to say, local authorities can expand the structure of opportunities for engagement by opening up their decision-making processes, and engaging in dialogue with representatives of community groups and voluntary organisations (Wallis and Dollery 2002). A survey of voluntary associations in Birmingham illustrates the way in which local public authorities have fostered the growth of community-based organisations since the 1981 Handsworth disturbances as a way of engaging with ethnic minority communities (Maloney *et al.* 2000a: 224). Of course, there is always a risk that partnership is dominated by the most articulate and most powerful (who will already be well connected).

In some areas, this has been associated with a wider change in the paradigms which shape the broadest level of policy. In the area of health, for example, the concept has played an important role in shifting health promotion strategies away from a individualistic model of health-related behaviour and simplistic psychologically-based models of learning, towards approaches that acknowledge the role of contexts (Morrow 1999). Similarly with labour market policy, where the effect of network-building on job search is well established (see above, pages 51–3). Certainly there is evidence that a lack of social contacts helps perpetuate long-term unemployment and maintain 'ghetto poverty' (Korpi 2001: 168). A number of studies of the New Deal programme in the UK show that the prospects of job placement have been substantially enhanced by the systematic use of personal contacts, including schemes of personalised guidance and support, mentoring and buddying (e.g. Heenan 2002). Of course, social capital can only marshal resources where they already exist (Portes and Landolt 2000: 547; Wilkinson 1996). It is not a substitute for credit, infrastructure, education and skills, but it can increase their yield by reinforcing statutory with voluntary effort, and sanctioning malfeasance.

Woolcock has emphasised the importance of linking social capital – that is, ties that reach outside the community concerned – in leveraging resources at times of distress, particularly where caused by external shock (Woolcock 2001: 15). There is some evidence that such linking ties can be deliberately created. An evaluation of local regeneration projects undertaken on Merseyside with support from the European Commission reported that there had been some '"scaling up" of elements of social capital between communities and wider power structures and institutions', generating 'relations of trust between residents and professional agencies'

(Hibbitt *et al.* 2001: 159). Whether these ties survive the removal of external support mechanisms – in this instance, finance from the European Social Fund – is less clear.

Linking social capital may also be particularly important in communities divided along ethnic or religious lines. In Northern Ireland, for example, much community development work has historically been concerned with building social capital through single identity work, designed to build community confidence to a level where people are prepared to engage in the risky and painful process of attempting reconciliation across the two communities. Yet, as Brendan Murtagh has pointed out, this rests on a 'spurious and uncertain connection' between two quite different process, and the end result – intended or not – may be to build exclusive bonding forms of social capital. Murtagh himself has argued that 'limited community relations resources should be directed at a range of activities likely to create, reproduce or deepen a denser network of bridging social capital', despite the strong prospects of resistance from the leaders of the communities concerned (Murtagh 2002: 3). Similarly, the United Nations High Commission on Refugees warned in the early 1980s against placing isolated asylum seekers and refugees in areas where local people were themselves poor and unaided; rather, it has been suggested, strategies should be developed which bridge the communities, allowing refugees to function as an asset rather than a cost, without necessarily breaking up the existing social capital of groups of refugees (Loizos 2000: 140).

Linking social capital is also important in respect of cluster creation, particularly if the purpose of policy is to make some impact on smaller firms. In economic policy, network creation is relatively simple. Simple competitive pressures make it most unlikely that effective clusters will be sustained in the absence of outside intervention. A survey of small firm networks in Denmark, Italy and the USA found very few examples of firms coming spontaneously together; the authors also noted that the capacity to sustain networks once they were in place was extremely uncertain, in the absence of external support (Hanna and Walsh 2002: 204). In an exhaustive study of innovation and training in the small firms sector, Matlay notes the success of methods such as mentoring, barter systems and business breakfasts/lunches, some of which led ultimately to long-lasting alliances (Matlay 1997: 229).

Finally, government may also use its capacity for promoting innovation to test new approaches to building connectedness. The most obvious area for experiment is surely the application of Information and Communications

Technologies (ICTs) to establish connections between people, particularly perhaps in remote, rural and island communities. The case of Netville, a newly wired suburb near Toronto, is instructive; here, universal access to high-speed Internet access helped bring neighbours together more frequently than in unwired areas, but also helped residents organise campaigns against the real estate developer and the local telecommunications company (Wellman and Hampton 1999). ICT can support new forms of public consultation, help people to share information and ideas, reduce barriers to economic transactions, and assist networking between groups who are sometimes excluded by more conventional means (OECD 2001b: 69; Ferlander and Timms 2001). However, there are also implications in more established fields of policy such as civic architecture and urban planning. The extent to which a community expects to influence behaviour in its local public space seems to be a major factor in fields such as the control of crime and disorder (Sampson and Raudenbush 1999). Again, there are obvious possibilities for innovative and experimental approaches to urban living that overcome some of the unintended consequences of urban ghettoisation in the past.

This by no means exhausts all the difficulties inherent in the project of applying the concept in practice. Some continue to argue that the scholarly debate does not seem to have produced anything so far which would justify clear policy signals. Alejandro Portes and Patricia Landolt have warned with respect to development policy that for the most part, 'the research literature has not been supportive of attempts at "social engineering" that seek to build solidary networks where few or none exist', opting instead for an approach designed to 'reinforce existing social ties and work alongside the definitions of the situation of community members' (Portes and Landolt 2000: 546). In particular, building bridging social capital may prove a greater challenge than at first appears. After all, the capacity to cooperate across weak bridging ties rests very substantially on people's ability to deal with others who are not similar to themselves, and who therefore bring resources that are not otherwise easily available from close connections. People involved for the first time in extended contacts with bridging ties may need to learn a 'command of variety'. A study of dining out among British businessmen and -women showed that the 'cultural omnivore' was able to draw on more sources of conversation in order to build wider networks and thus benefit from a wider circulation of knowledge (Warde *et al.* 1999: 122). To apply this insight to inner-city communities or to the population of island and remote regions, who in the past have developed reasonably successful coping strategies on the basis of their close bonding ties, may not be a simple matter.

A second set of problems arises from the dark side of social capital. Promoting stronger networks and shared norms is not only difficult to achieve, but the strengthening of existing ties may create opportunities for cronyism within the community affected, and reduce the prospects of linkages to resources that are available outside its ranks. In a critical appraisal of the World Bank's role in Mexico, Jonathan Fox concluded that it was paying for social programmes that were slowing down the democratisation process and reinforcing the patronage of violent bosses, and thereby 'contributing, on balance, to the *dismantling* of social capital' (Fox 1997: 971). The World Bank has tried to address this problem by adopting Woolcock's distinction between bridging social capital and bonding social capital as a way of directing its decisions:

> A key lesson for practitioners and policy makers is the importance of using existing forms of bridging social capital in poor communities as a basis for scaling up the efforts of local community-based organisations.
> (World Bank 2001: 130; see also Woolcock 2001)

However, this is not always easy, particularly given that the prosperous and well-educated are much more likely to participate in civic activities than are the least advantaged (see Chapter 3, pages 75–6). Policy should, therefore, focus not only on the amount of civic activity but also its distribution.

In the end, though policy can certainly be devised to support social capital, it has limits. Apart from anything else, most of the features of social capital are not really open to external intervention. Most of the policy literature emphasises formal ties, often between organisations or neighbourhoods, such as buyer–supplier relationships and joint ventures in the case of economic policy, or public–private partnerships and voluntary–statutory linkages in the case of social policy. But recent research has tended to find that cooperation in a number of policy fields is often facilitated by 'many types of informal, interpersonal relationships' such as kinship and friendship connections (Ingram and Roberts 2000: 388). And these are not something that governments or employers or community leaders can easily create. They can bring people together, and ensure that the conditions exist for instrumental cooperation. They cannot force people to like each other, fall in love, or enjoy time in each other's company – and then go the extra mile in terms of trust and regard.

CAN GOVERNMENTS CREATE SOCIAL CAPITAL?

The obstacles to successful policy are, then, many. But this does not mean that the search for relevant policy is a dead-end. Apart from anything else, government policies already affect social capital, or are formulated without taking it into account. This can be particularly harmful where policies are adopted which damage the social capital of particularly vulnerable people. For example, Peter Loizos has warned that policies which ignore or disrupt the social capital of refugees can inflict additional penalties upon them (Loizos 2000: 126). In a number of countries, governments are allowing the construction of high-security estates surrounded by fencing and monitored by closed circuit cameras (Harper 2001: 20), but while helping build social capital among residents, these can prevent the formation of bridging ties with other people outside the estate, which in turn makes crime more likely. Government action can, then, inadvertently end up by destroying social capital, and reducing people's capacity for cooperation to tackle problems. At the most negative, then, it is prudent for government to ensure that it seeks to do as little harm as possible to people's stocks of social capital, unless it can be sure that they are using their connections mainly for perverse ends. Even then, it may be better for government to be aware that it is dealing with networks underpinned by shared norms, and not simply with isolated individuals.

Probably the best role for government is to serve as an enabler, and then stand back. The Time Bank initiative in the UK is a good example of the way that policy-makers can promote association, without worrying too much about the details (Harper 2001: 22). Supported in part by the Home Office, Time Banks have been declared exempt from tax, and also from welfare benefit consideration, so that unemployed people and others on benefits can volunteer their services without fear of punishment. The kinds of services offered include gardening, companionship, shopping, computer tuition and help with literacy skills. Scandinavian policies designed to create high-technology clusters, bringing together research centres and the business sector to work on innovative R & D projects, with a mix of public and private funding, can also continue with a relatively low level of direct state involvement (Maskell and Törnqvist 1999). Common Purpose, a British not-for-profit organisation created by Julia Middleton with the aim of strengthening networks among civic decision-takers, has deliberately avoided attracting support from government as a way of maintaining its political and organisational independence.

On balance, then, government has to strike a delicate balance. On the one hand, it would be foolhardy for any policy-maker to ignore social capital altogether. Apart from anything else, the implementation of policies in almost any area will be influenced by the networks found among the various policy actors involved (who typically might include business leaders, civil servants and politicians). Once the policy is being implemented, its results will be influenced by the social capital of those at whom the policy is aimed (including any associations claiming to represent them). More ambitious programmes to promote social capital are bound to be attractive to governments who are seeking not just to provide services to people, but to engage them in changing behaviour and values in respect of such policy fields as public health, environmental protection or lifelong learning. Yet in developing policies which favour social capital investment, government also needs to avoid the risks of either inadvertently undermining existing sources of social capital, or of producing connections that have more negative than positive consequences. And since research on social capital is still at a relatively early stage of development, it is simply not possible at this stage to predict with any confidence whether more ambitious measures will achieve their goals.

CONCLUSION

Social capital began as a comparatively simple concept, and it has evolved rapidly into a rather more complex account of people's relationships and their value. Yet as the debate has developed, it has become increasingly clear that the original conceptualisations of social capital are limited and possibly flawed. As developed by Bourdieu, Coleman and Putnam, the initial conceptions remain somewhat sketchy and loose; in the hands of others, they have been stretched to fit a wide variety of hypotheses and models. Much of the evidence and discussion reviewed in this book has confirmed that the concept has at least some heuristic value, as an open concept designed to guide further investigation (Schuller *et al.* 2000). Further, the debate over social capital has started to lay bare some of the ways in which social ties can be activated to produce particular types of benefit (Dika and Singh 2002), as well as the ways in which it can produce negative outcomes or reinforce inequality (see Chapter 3). Yet there are also reasons for suggesting that more needs to be done before the concept can be said to have achieved any kind of theoretical maturity.

After all, the very idea of social capital has been widely contested. Some have questioned its *coherence*: that is, whether the term refers to a linked, definable and consistent set of behaviours and relationships, or whether it is – as Warde and Tampubolon suggest – a 'chaotic concept' (Bankston and Zhou 2002; Portes 1998; Robison *et al.* 2002; Warde and Tampubolon 2002: 177). It is certainly possible to find examples of loose and even inconsistent usages of the concept, but this is always the case when any social theory starts to spread beyond a small group of like-minded specialists. The more important aspect of this objection concerns the extent to which the concept really refers to activities, relationships and values that are linked to one another. Of course, the same criticism can easily be levelled against many other terms, such as social class or human capital, but that is not much of an argument on behalf of social capital's coherence. My own view is that its coherence is really a question for empirical research. At present, we are still in the earliest stages of serious empirical investigation of social capital; while the available evidence suggests that the concept does indeed point to a coherent set of variables, we cannot yet be confident that this is the case, nor do we really have a clear sense as yet of its boundaries.

A further set of concerns relates to the *language* in which the concept is expressed. In particular, a number of scholars have asked whether the term 'capital' can really be justified. Social networks lack obvious properties of capital, such as reducibility to a common currency, substitutability, transferability and opportunities for direct investment (Robison *et al.* 2002). From a broadly Foucauldian perspective, some critics suggest that the historical association of the term with conventional economic discourses has important ideological consequences, and helps blur crucial issues of power and control (Blaxter and Hughes 2001; Smith and Kulynch 2002). Others take issue with the concept on rather different grounds, questioning whether it is possible to regard networks and norms as a form of capital at all (Cohen 1999). After all, the essential quality of capital is the fact that it is transferable; and, in the end, its transferability rests on its reduction to cash. Yet even though it cannot readily be translated into cash terms, social capital does have at least as high a degree of transferability (or fungibility) as human capital. Taking Putnam's definition, the least transferable dimension of social capital is trust, which in its interpersonal form is 'by definition specific and contextual' (Cohen 1999: 220). But I have argued previously that trust is a product of social capital, not one of its components. As Woolcock argues, trust and reciprocity 'are nurtured in and by particular combinations of social relationships . . . but they do not exist independently of social relationships' (Woolcock 1998: 185). In defining social capital, the focus must be on the sources rather than solely or even mainly the consequences. In exploring the ways in which the consequences arise, we need to attend not only to the components of social capital, but also to the ways in which it is activated (Dika and Singh 2002).

However, it is the consequences that enable us to use the term capital. Social capital can be termed capital in so far as it gives rise to resources that can be deployed in order to enable actors – both individuals and groups – to pursue their goals more effectively than they could without it. To try to read much more into the terminology is likely to lead down a labyrinth of simile. At least in principle, this pragmatic usage should allow for a variety of different theoretical frameworks to bear on the concept. For example, radical critics should be able to work with and through the language of capital in the domain of human relationships just as effectively (or ineffectively) as they do in other domains.

Of course, the metaphor of capital can only be taken so far. Other forms of capital can usually be bought and sold in the market, and are therefore mediated by money. Financial capital, physical capital and even human capital can be given a cash price, and can be traded against other commodities in the market place. Social networks, on the other hand, are not so readily translated into the language of the market place. Nor can they be traded against other commodities. As Coleman pointed out, a social network derives its strength from its context: 'A given form of social capital that is valuable in facilitating certain actions may be useless or even harmful for others' (Coleman 1994: 302). But Coleman also pointed out that physical and human capital are also less than wholly 'fungible' (Coleman 1994: 302), so that a skilled shipwright cannot simply be substituted for a nurse, nor a battleship for a film projector.

Others have questioned the *need* for the concept, arguing that the insights attributed to social capital analyses are already well established (Portes 1998: 21). From this perspective, the advocates of the concept are simply reinventing – or even just renaming – the wheel. I have already shown on a number of occasions that many of the phenomena associated with social capital had already been noticed, in a tradition of social analysis going back at least as far as Durkheim and possibly even further. Nevertheless, this is in itself no reason for abandoning the concept, any more than we might dump the category of social class just because it existed before Marx came along. What may be more significant is the challenge to demonstrate that the concept really does bring something new and distinctive to the debate. In this volume, I have tried to bring together the literature from a variety of fields, many of which employ subtly different approaches to the study of networks and norms; for example, Chapter 2 explored the work undertaken in educational studies, much of which is deeply influenced by Coleman, alongside studies of the labour market or business growth, which has tended to draw on concepts of social capital that are drawn from economic sociology (Burt 1992; Lin 2001). Clearly there are benefits to be gained from comparing work carried out using different perspectives, though there is also a risk of absorbing without thought the results of earlier research that was conducted under different labels.

Finally, there is a group who object mainly to the *politics* associated with social capital (Avis 2002; Blaxter and Hughes 2001: 85–7; Fine 2000). This group complains that the main reason that policy-makers and professionals are so enthusiastic about social capital is because it subordinates the social to the economic. In particular, they are prone to use the term to justify a retreat from welfare spending. Further, there is a risk that policy-makers may adopt the language of social capital as part of what has been called 'deficit theory', claiming that unsuccessful families and communities are failing because they lack the 'right' networks (Morrow 1999: 760). Of course, this can be true of almost any resource that we care to mention. It is easy to blame the poor for their own poverty, and it is as important to avoid this pitfall in the case of social capital as in other respects. Nor should we allow an interest in social capital to distract us from other structural factors which determine people's life chances. Network poverty may contribute to social exclusion and disadvantage, but it is wrong to ignore the material basis of poverty. A meaningful notion of social capital needs to be used in ways that also recognise other social, economic, cultural and political forces.

What social capital brings to social theory is an emphasis on relationships and values as significant factors in explaining structures and behaviour. To be more precise, it contributes new insights by focussing on what two of the more thoughtful critics describe as 'meso level social structures' such as family, neighbourhood, voluntary associations and public institutions as integrating elements between individuals and wider social structures (Edwards and Foley 1997: 677). Moreover, it allows social scientists to examine the role of these meso-level structures in a systematic way. While it certainly has enormous value as a heuristic device, then, this volume has also presented abundant evidence that social capital actually affects the outcomes of social behaviour, and can therefore reasonably be considered as a variable in its own right.

Social capital must be understood as a relational construct. It can only provide access to resources where individuals have not only formed ties with others but have internalised the shared values of the group. For this reason, it is important to treat the concept as a property of relationships.

This perhaps implies more of a return to Durkheimian concerns with social solidarity, rather than following Coleman's elegantly individualist framework. Coleman's work has been widely criticised for sharing with rational choice theory a highly individualistic, and calculating, model of human behaviour. Rational choice theory assumes that participation in collective behaviour represents a deviation from the norm, which consists of individuals pursuing their own private interests, if necessary at the expense of others. Cooperation and trust are therefore aberrations, and rational choice theorists believe that individuals only embrace collective action where they think this is the best way of achieving their individual choices. One group of economists, for instance, has defined social capital as a largely individual quality, consisting of 'a person's social characteristics – including social skills, charisma, and the size of his Rolodex – which enable him to reap market and non-market returns from interactions with others' (Glaeser *et al*. 2002: 438). In short, people only cooperate when they believe that they will gain from doing so. In so far as they invest in their capacity to cooperate with others, they can be said to be building up their individual social capital.

Rational choice theories of social capital should not be dismissed out of hand. Apart from anything else, they provide a useful counterbalance to those who overestimate the importance of structure and downplay the role of agency. People do indeed make conscious choices to invest in their social capital, and these decisions can be influenced by the existence of private incentives (such as home ownership) for doing so. Moreover, rational choice theory lends itself to the economic analysis of social capital, with its attention to questions of investment and returns. There is, then, likely to be be continued interest in rational choice as an overarching theory for further research.

Rational choice theory has also been widely criticised, particularly among sociologists. It has been attacked, for instance, for a lack of attention to norms and shared meaning – in other words, for culture – as an ever-present facet of social life. It is not simply that humans are influenced by their values and attitudes, and not only by their rational calculation of their individual interests. More recently, Misztal and Sztompka have both pointed out that rational choice theory has no place for affect – that is, for such basic elements of human behaviour as altruism, love and friendship (Misztal 1996: 80–8; Sztompka 1999: 66). And it is also highly vulnerable to the argument – often levelled against Coleman's work on education – that rational choice approaches to social capital systematically neglect the impact of material inequalities on people's lives. As well as an under-standing of agency, then, we need to remain attentive to the constraints and opportunities that are presented by group norms and social structures.

If social capital is seen as relational, it embraces more than the indi-vidual level of behaviour. It must be understood as an attribute of the individual (in relation to others), and of the collectivity. Both Bourdieu and Coleman tended to treat social capital as something which delivered benefits to its individual owners, in the form of reliable expectations about the behaviour of others. Putnam has clearly extended the concept to apply to groups, from league bowling teams and choirs to states and nations. He has been criticised for the degree of 'conceptual stretch' involved, partly because he has never explicitly theorised it as such and partly because he has tangled cause and effect together (Portes and Landolt 2000: 535–7). But perhaps this is to seek too much neatness. Pierre Bourdieu is wonderfully clear about the cause (elite networks) and the effects (maintenance and improvement of elite status), but does this help much? It is better to see the process as iterative and multiplex, with constant reinvestment and occasional disinvestment, and with many forms of networks not only delivering positive benefits, but themselves constituting a positive outcome for actors. Gang membership confers esteem and builds confidence among disenfranchised young males, anxious to earn 'respect'. Golf clubs are a place to enjoy the company of friends, and to make new friends.

Social capital is a differentiated phenomenon: it varies in its components, in its liquidity, and in the contexts in which it is found (Foley and Edwards 1999). Coleman and Putnam in particular have tended to emphasise the importance of horizontal linkages, and largely neglected power inequalities. Vivien Lowndes notes that they have generally neglected care-based networks, which typically are built by women, precisely because the social capital they create is not usually convertible into access to formal politics and business leadership (Lowndes 2000: 536). Yet possession of social capital in itself by no means guarantees equality of access to social and economic resources. Knowing a range of other people and being able to cooperate with them is obviously a good way of making things happen, but just how much will happen depends on the resources that those other people control. To generalise, poor people mostly live next door to other poor people; travelling people tend to marry the sons and daughters of travelling people; women enjoy networking with other women. Conversely, old Etonians often assume that other old Etonians can generally be relied on; Freemasons do favours for other Freemasons; eminent scientists attend conferences and seminars with other top people from their own discipline. Equally, outsiders can sometimes assume that inside connections are at work even if they are not. The contemporary Scottish folk hero and anti-toll bridge campaigner, Robbie the Pict, complains that Scotland's judges are reaching what he views as biassed decisions not because this is an inherent feature of the law of property, but because they belong to a secret Edinburgh dining club (*The Scotsman*, 17 December 2002). Popular perceptions of power and powerlessness often arise from awareness of connections and their importance, yet at times the perceived importance of 'old boy' networks can distract attention from underlying and more structural inequalities.

Of course, powerless and poor communities can sometimes draw on their reserves of social capital to compensate for their lack of status and wealth. Indeed, that is precisely the purpose of many social movements, such as trade unions, and it helps explain why trust-based institutions of the poor – like credit unions – can function. One response to the differentiation of social capital might be to map the different dimensions and varying consequences. It is clear that the social capital arising from associational membership has different results from that derived from friendship ties, and this presumably reflects the qualities associated with the ties themselves (Warde and Tampubolon 2002). But often, the inequalities of access to reserves of social capital will intersect with other inequalities, such as those of wealth or gender or ethnicity. And often, the dominant literature on social capital has simply not recognised this fact.

As well as conceptual challenges, there are also important questions of method in researching social capital. Much current research is based on communal measures of civic engagement and norms, as in Putnam's use of data from the General Social Survey. Yet these data, while illuminating for some purposes, do not really offer much evidence on the nature and quality of people's connections. Network analysis offers one possible solution. The methods used in this approach have the merit of being tried and tested, having evolved steadily since the 1950s. Conventionally, much network analysis proceeds through the use of name generators – that is, by asking subjects to identify the names of individuals whom they know particularly well – and then using the results to map the complex networks of relationships between individuals (Scott 1991; Degenne and Fossé 1999).

Work within economic sociology has sought to bring this method to bear upon the debate over social capital. Nan Lin in particular has argued for a marriage of rational choice theory with network analysis as a basis for investigating social capital (Lin 2001). Yet this method has also been criticised for risking over-emphasising the role of strong ties. In an attempt to overcome this limitation, Zhao (2002) has explored the alternative of position indicators, asking actors to name individuals that they encounter through particular episodes (in this case, whom actors chose to visit during a Chinese festival). Network analysis has produced a body of research methods, and categories of analysis, that have been developed in order to study informal as well as formal relationships (Wasserman and Faust 1994). It is of course far from being the only option – for example, Durlauf (2002) has recommended greater use of experimental data – but it offers considerable potential for future studies of social capital.

Previous chapters have explored a number of areas where there is now a reasonably robust base of empirical evidence, as well as many others where our knowledge is at best sketchy and uneven. There is a growing body of work which draws on qualitative and ethnographic data, though as yet there has been no published work which draws systematically on life history methods to examine individuals' changing bonds over time. There is an expanding volume of quantitative studies; to these may be added some of the official surveys noted in Chapter 5 that now include units on social capital. There is an emerging body of work on the gender dynamics of social capital, which, it has been suggested, has the potential for broadening the terms in which the debate is conducted to embrace a wider set of networks, and challenging the 'public/private' split that dominates much political science (Lowndes 2000). Whether this will really shed as much light as Lowndes claims on the causal links at work in what she describes as 'the virtuous circle of social capital' (Lowndes 2000: 536) remains to be seen. However, it certainly opens up the prospect of debate over a wider set of connections than those which have so far dominated most of the published accounts.

Future research will also need to pay attention to the way in which people activate their social capital. Coleman's conceptualisation in particular has been criticised for confusing the sources of social capital (relationships) with the benefits (resources), and failing to disentangle possession of social capital from its activation (Dika and Singh 2002). This appears to be a promising line of enquiry. One study of the use of intermediaries by individuals in an organisation in order to achieve their goals showed that individuals mobilised their networks in a differentiated and selective manner, which varied depending on the type of social capital, the 'owner' of the reserves, and the relationships between the protagonists (Lazega and

Lebeaux 1995). However, even within this single study it was also possible to discern other factors at work, including the organisational culture and the identities of the people concerned. Evidently this is a complex subject, and one which is likely to receive considerable attention as the debate unfolds. Social capital, though, continues to look a rich terrain for future research.

Research and scholarship are important, but the idea of social capital is also of direct relevance to the way that people live their lives. Anthony Giddens points out that the pervasive reflexivity of high modernity arises at least in part because people take up ideas from the social sciences and apply them to their own conditions of existence (Giddens 1991). Social capital, I have suggested, is a useful way of looking at people's relationships with one another at least in part because it can be and is operationalised by policy-makers and others. But what does this mean in our late modern world, where utopian ideas of what it means to lead a good life have fragmented?

In so far as people imagine life in terms of a common good, their preference is increasingly for communities based on achieved characteristics over those based on ascribed characteristics. In less sociological terms, they are ever less likely to think of the communities in which they are thrown by accident of birth or habit, and ever more likely to think in terms of the communities to which they choose to belong, or even have helped directly to create. One British study showed that although relationships are becoming somewhat more fluid and even reflexive in nature, it was precisely these qualities that made them increasingly central to adults' identities (Pahl and Spencer 1997: 103). Rather than bowling in organised leagues, playing against teams from neighbouring suburbs or factories, people prefer to drive to the alley to play with family or friends (possibly after arranging the match by email), and might have quite a different and varying network of people whom they meet in the pub or in the fitness centre. Moreover, they might lose interest in bowling entirely, and take up golf or hill-walking instead.

Our relationships have changed, and are still changing. And similarly, our relationship with our relationships is changing. In a more secular, individualised, informal and networked yet less easily legible and transparent world, we should heed Barbara Misztal's advice:

> to have the upper hand, to ensure safe passage and to prove one's knowledge of the rules, one needs to develop increasingly sophisticated

skills of reading and interpreting symbols and signs that others exhibit in everyday life.

(Misztal 1996: 116)

Habit and conformity provide poor guides to the future, whether in our intimate relationships, in our wider networks of friendship and acquaintance, or in our connections at work. Indeed, reliance on habit may be worse than useless; it may actively create disillusion on the part of another who believes we are taking them 'for granted'. If this creates difficulties, they are probably not those normally meant by people who lament the decline of community. Rather, they are the difficulties of negotiating a reflexive life while all around you are doing the same, in the absence of fixed coordinates to provide as basis for navigation through the fog. Perhaps there should be a national programme for social literacy, not only for school children but also – and maybe primarily – for adults.

REFERENCES

Aguilera, M. A. (2002) 'The Impact of Social Capital on Labor Force Participation: evidence from the 2000 Social Capital Benchmark Survey', *Social Science Quarterly*, 83, 3, 853–74.

Alheit, P. (1996) 'Research and Innovation in Contemporary Adult Education', in S. Papaioannou, P. Alheit, J. F. Lauridsen and H. S. Olesen (eds), *Community, Education and Social Change*, Roskilde University Centre, Roskilde.

Allatt, P. (1993) 'Becoming Privileged: the role of family process', in I. Bates and G. Riseborough (eds), *Youth and Inequality*, Open University Press, Buckingham.

Althusser, L. (1977) *For Marx*, New Left Books, London.

Avis, J. (2002) 'Social Capital, Collective Intelligence and Expansive Learning: thinking through the connections', *British Journal of Educational Studies*, 50, 3, 308–26.

Banfield, E. (1958) *The Moral Basis of a Backwards Society*, Free Press, Chicago.

Bankston, C. L. and Zhou, M. (2002) 'Social Capital as Process: the meanings and problems of a theoretical metaphor', *Sociological Inquiry*, 72, 2, 285–317.

Baron, J. N., Hannan, M. T. and Burton, M. D. (2001) 'Labor Pains: change in organisational models and employee turnover in young, high-tech firms', *American Journal of Sociology*, 106, 4, 960–1012.

Baron, S., Field, J. and Schuller, T. (eds) (2000) *Social Capital: critical perspectives*, Oxford University Press, Oxford.

Bates, T. (1994) 'Social Resources Generated by Group Support Networks May not be Beneficial to Asian Immigrant-owned Small Businesses', *Social Forces*, 72, 3, 671–89.

Beck, U. (2000) 'Living Your Own Life in a Runaway World: individualisation, globalisation and politics', pp. 164–74, in W. Hutton and A. Giddens (eds), *On the Edge: living with global capitalism*, Jonathan Cape, London.

Beck, U. and Beck-Gernsheim, E. (1994) *Riskante Freiheiten: Individualisierung in modernen Gesellschaften*, Suhrkamp, Franktfurt-am-Main.

Beck, U. and Beck-Gernsheim, E. (2002) *Individualisation: individualised individualism and its social and political consequences*, Sage, London.

Becker, G. S. (1964) *Human Capital: a theoretical and empirical analysis*, New York: National Bureau of Economic Research.

Blair, T. (2001) 'Third Way, Phase Two', *Prospect*, 61, 10–13.

Blaxter, L. and Hughes, C. (2001) 'Social Capital: a critique', in J. Thompson (ed.), *Stretching the Academy: the politics and practice of widening participation in higher education*, Leicester, National Institute for Adult Continuing Education.

Bockmeyer, J. L. (2000) 'A Culture of Distrust: the impact of local political culture on participation in the Detroit EZ', *Urban Studies*, 37, 13, 2417–40.

Boehnke, K., Hagan, J. and Merkens, H. (2000) 'Right-wing Extremism among German Adolescents: risk factors and protective factors', *Applied Psychology*, 47, 1, 109–26.

Boisjoly, J., Duncan, G. and Hofferth, S. (1995) 'Access to Social Capital', *Journal of Family Issues*, 16, 5, 609–31.

Bourdieu, P. (1977) 'Cultural Reproduction and Social Reproduction', pp. 487–511 in J. Karabel and A. H. Halsey (eds) *Power and Ideology in Education*, Oxford University Press, New York.

Bourdieu, P. (1980) 'Le capital social: notes provisoires', *Actes de la récherche en sciences sociales*, 2–3.

Bourdieu, P. (1981) 'Ökonomisches Kapital, Kulturelles Kapital, soziales Kapital', in R. Kreckel (ed.) *Soziale Ungleichheiten*, Otto Schartz, Göttingen.

Bourdieu, P. (1984) *Distinction: a social critique of the judgement of taste*, Routledge, London.

Bourdieu, P. (1986) 'The Forms of Capital', pp 241–58 in J. G. Richardson (ed.), *Handbook of Theory and Research for the Sociology of Education*, Greenwood Press, New York.

Bourdieu, P. (1988) *Homo Academicus*, Polity Press, Cambridge.

Bourdieu, P. and Passeron, J.-C. (1977) *Reproduction in Education, Society and Culture*, London: Sage.

Bourdieu, P. and Wacquant, L. (1992) *An Invitation to Reflexive Sociology*, Chicago, University of Chicago Press.

Brettell, B. C. (2000) 'Theorising Migration in Anthropology', pp. 97–135 in B. C. Brettell and F. J. Hollifield (eds), *Migration Theory: talking across disciplines*, Routledge, London.

Burt, R. (1992) *Structural Holes: the social structure of competition*, Cambridge, Harvard University Press.

Busse, S. (2001) 'Post-Soviet Social Capital: evidence from ethnography', Paper presented at American Sociological Association Annual Meeting, Anaheim, California.

Caligiuri, M. P., Joshi, A. and Lazarova, M. (1999) 'Factors Influencing the Appointment of Women on Global Assignments', *International Journal of Human Resource Management*, 10, 2, 163–79.

Campbell, C. (2000) 'Social Capital and Health: contextualising health promotion within local community networks', pp. 182–96 in S. Baron, J. Field. and T. Schuller (eds), *Social Capital: critical perspectives*, Oxford University Press, Oxford.

Campbell, C. and McLean, C. (2002) 'Ethnic Identities, Social Capital and Health Inequalities: factors shaping African-Caribbean participation in local community networks in the UK', *Social Science and Medicine*, 55, 4, 643–57.

Cambell, C., Wood, R. and Kelly, M. (1999) *Social Capital and Health*, Health Education Authority, London.

Castells, M. (1996) *The Information Age, Volume 1: the rise of the network society*, Basil Blackwell, Oxford.

Champlin, D. (1999) 'Social Capital and the Privatisation of Public Goods', *International Journal of Social Economics*, 26, 10/11, 1302–14.

Chiricos, T., McEntire, R. and Gertz, M. (2001) 'Perceived Ethnic and Racial Composition of Neighbourhood and Perceived Risk of Crime', *Social Problems*, 48, 3, 322–40.

Clark, E. (2000) 'The Role of Social Capital in Developing Czech Private Business', *Work, Employment and Society*, 14, 3, 439–58.

Cohen, J. (1999) 'Trust, Voluntary Association and Workable Democracy: the contemporary American discourse of civil society', pp. 208–48 in M. E. Warren (ed.) *Democracy and Trust*, Cambridge University Press, Cambridge.

Coleman, J. S. (1961) *Adolescent Society: the social life of the teenager and its impact on education*, Free Press, New York.

Coleman, J. S. (1988–9) 'Social Capital in the Creation of Human Capital', *American Journal of Sociology*, 94, 95–120.

Coleman, J. S. (1990) *Equality and Achievement in Education*, Westview Press, Boulder.

Coleman, J. S. (1991) 'Prologue: constructed social organisation', pp. 1–14 in P. Bourdieu and J. S. Coleman (eds), *Social Theory for a Changing Society*, Westview Press, Boulder.

Coleman, J. S. (1994) *Foundations of Social Theory*, Belknap Press, Cambridge MA.

Coleman, J. S., Campbell, E. Q., Hobson, C. J., McPartland, J., Mood, A.M., Weinfeld, F. D. and York, R. L. (1966) *Equality of Educational Opportunity*, Washington, United States Government Printing Office.

Coleman, J. S., Hoffer, T. and Kilgore, S. (1982) *High School Achievement: public, Catholic and Private Schools Compared*, Basic Books, New York.

Coleman, J. S. and Hoffer, T. (1987) *Public and Private Schools: the impact of communities*, Basic Books, New York.

Commission for Social Justice (1994) *Social Justice: strategies for national renewal*, Vintage, London.

Cooper, H., Arber, S., Fee, L. and Ginn, J. (1999) *The Influence of Social Support and Social Capital on Health: a review and analysis of British data*, Health Education Authority, London.

Dahrendorf, R. (1990) *Reflections on the Revolution in Europe*, Chatto and Windus, London.

Dasgupta, P. (2000) 'Economic Progress and the Idea of Social Capital', pp. 325–424 in P. Dasgupta and I. Serageldin (eds), *Social Capital: a multifaceted perspective*, World Bank, Washington DC.

Davies, J. K. (2001) 'Partnership Working in Health Promotion: the potential role of social capital in health development', pp. 181–200 in Ballock, S. and Taylor, M. (eds) *Partnership Working: policy and practice*, Policy Press, Bristol.

De Tocqueville, A. (1832) [1969] *Democracy in America*, Harper, New York.

Dean, M. (1999) *Governmentality: power and rule in modern society*, Sage, London.

Degenne, A. and Fossé, M. (1999) *Introducing Social Networks*, Sage, London.

Dhesi, A. S. (2000) 'Social Capital and Community Development', *Community Development Journal*, 35, 3, 199–214.

Dika, S. L. and Singh, K. (2002) 'Applications of Social Capital in Educational Literature: a critical synthesis', *Review of Educational Research*, 72, 1, 31–60.

Dowley, K. M. and Silver, B. D. (2002) 'Social Capital, Ethnicity and Support for Democracy in the Post-Communist States', *Europe-Asia Studies*, 54, 4, 505–27.

Durkheim, Emile. 1933. *The Division of Labor in Society*, Translated by George Simpson, The Free Press, New York.

Durlauf, S. N. (2002) 'On the Empirics of Social Capital', *The Economic Journal*, 112, 459–79.

Edwards, B. and Foley, M. (1997) 'Social Capital and the Political Economy of our Discontent', *American Behavioural Scientist*, 40, 5, 669–78.

Emler, N. and McNamara, S. (1996) 'The Social Contact Patterns of Young People: effects of participation in the social institutions of family, education and work', pp. 121–39 in H. Helve and J. Bynner (eds), *Youth and Life Management: research perspectives*, Yliopistopaino, Helsinki.

Employment Department (1996) *Managing Careers in the 21st Century*, Skills and Enterprise Briefing, 4/96, 3.

Esbensen, F.-A, Deschenes, E.P., and Winfree, L.T. (1999) 'Differences Between Gang Girls and Gang Boys: results from a multisite survey', *Youth and Society*, 31, 1, 27–53.

Etzioni, A. (1993) *The Spirit of Community: rights, responsibilities and the communitarian agenda*, Fontana, London.

Fafchamps, M., and Minten, B. (2002) 'Returns to Social Network Capital among Traders', *Oxford Economic Papers*, 54, 2, 173–206.

Ferlander, S. and Timms, D. (2001) 'Local Nets and Social Capital', *Telematics and Informatics*, 18, 51–65.

Fernandez, R.M., Castilla, E. J. and Moore, P. (2000) 'Social Capital at Work: networks and employment at a phone center', *American Journal of Sociology*, 105, 5, 1288–356.

Ferrary, M. (2002) 'Mécanismes de régulation de la structure des qualifications et specificité du capital human. Une analyse du capital social des conseillers bancaires', *Sociologie du Travail*, 44, 1, 119–30.

Field, J. and Schuller, T. (2000) 'Networks, Norms and Trust: explaining patterns of lifelong learning in Scotland and Northern Ireland', pp. 95–118, in F. Coffield (ed.), *Differing Visions of the Learning Society: research findings 2*, Policy Press, Bristol.

Field, J. and Spence, L. (2000) 'Social Capital and Informal Learning', pp. 32–42 in F. Coffield (ed.), *The Necessity of Informal Learning*, Policy Press, Bristol.

Fine, B. (2000) *Social Capital versus Social Theory: political economy and social science at the turn of the millenium*, Routledge, London.

Fine, B. and Green, F. (2000) 'Economics, Social Capital, and the Colonisation of the Social Sciences', pp. 78–93 in S. Baron, J. Field and T. Schuller (eds), *Social Capital: critical perspectives*, Oxford University Press, Oxford.

Foley, M. and Edwards, B. (1999) 'Is it Time to Disinvest in Social Capital?' *Journal of Public Policy*, 19, 2, 141–73.

Fox, J. (1997) 'The World Bank and Social Capital: contesting the concept in practice', *Journal of International Development*, 9, 7, 963–71.

Fukuyama, F. (1989) 'The End of History', Lecture at the University of Chicago, accessed on 1 September 2002 at http://www.wku.edu/~sullib/history.htm

Fukuyama, F. (1995) *Trust: the social virtues and the creation of prosperity*, Hamish Hamilton, London.

Fukuyama, F. (2001) 'Social Capital, Civil Society and Development', *Third World Quarterly*, 22, 1, 7–20.

Furedi, F. (2002) 'For the Greater Good of my CV', *Times Higher Educational Supplement*, 27 September 2002, 24–5.

Gardner, J. and Oswad, A. (2002) *Internet Use: the digital divide*, Working Paper, Department of Economics, University of Warwick, Coventry.

Gershuny, J. (2001) 'Web-use and Net-nerds: a neo-functionalist analysis of the impact of information technology in the home', Conference of the International Association for Time Use Research, Oslo, 3–5 October 2001.

Gershuny, J., and Fisher, K. (1999) *Leisure in the UK Across the 20th Century*, Institute for Social and Economic Research Working Paper 99–3, University of Essex, Colchester.

Giddens, A. (1984) *The Constitution of Society*, Polity, Cambridge.

Giddens, A. (1991) *Modernity and Self-identity: self and the society in the late modern age*, Polity, Cambridge.

Glaeser, E. L. (2001) 'The Formation of Social Capital', pp. 381–93 in J. F. Helliwell (ed.) *The Contribution of Human and Social Capital to Sustained Economic Growth and Well-Being*, Human Resources Development Canada/Organisation for Economic Co-operation and Growth, Ottawa/Paris.

Glaeser, E. L., Laibson, D. and Sacerdote, B. (2002) 'An Economic Approach to Social Capital', *The Economic Journal*, 112, 437–58.

Glaeser, E. L., Laibson, D. I., Scheinkman, J. and Soutter, C. L. (2000) 'Measuring Trust', *Quarterly Journal of Economics*, 115, 811–46.

Granovetter, M. (1973) 'The Strength of Weak Ties', *American Journal of Sociology*, 78, 1360–80.

Green, G., Grimsley, M., Suokas, A., Prescott, M., Jowitt, T. and Linacre, R. (2000) *Social Capital, Health and Economy in South Yorkshire Coalfield Communities*, Centre for Regional Economic and Social Research, Sheffield.

Grootaert, C. (1996) 'Social Capital, the Missing Link?' in *Monitoring Environmental Progress – Expanding the Measure of Wealth*, World Bank, Washington.

Groundwork (2002) 'News & Events', 19 August 2002, Accessed on 1 September 2002 at http://www.groundwork.org.uk/news/190802–FRINGEEVENTS.htm.

Hagan, J., MacMillan, R. and Wheaton, B. (1996) 'Social Capital and the Life Course Effects of Family Migration', *American Sociological Review*, 61, 3, 368–85.

Hall, P. (1999) 'Social Capital in Britain', *British Journal of Political Science*, 29, 3, 417–61.

Halpern, D. (2001) 'Moral Values, Social Trust and Inequality: can values explain crime?' *British Journal of Criminology*, 41, 2, 236–51.

Hanna, V. and Walsh, K. (2002) 'Small Firm Networks: a successful approach to innovation?' *R&D Management*, 32, 3, 201–7.

Harper, R. (2001) *Social Capital: a review of the literature*, Office for National Statistics, London.

Haynie, D. L. (2001) 'Delinquent Peers Revisited: does network structure matter?' *American Journal of Sociology*, 106, 4, 1013–57.

Heckman, J. J. and Neal, D. (1996) 'Coleman's Contributions to Education: theory, research styles and empirical research', pp. 81–102 in J. Clark (ed.) *James S. Coleman*, Falmer Press, London.

Hedoux, C. (1982) 'Des publics et des non-publics de la formation d'adults', *Revue française de sociologie*, 23, 253–74.

Heenan, D. (2002) '"It Won't Change the World But it Turned My Life Around": participants' views on the Personal Adviser Scheme in the New Deal for Disabled People', *Disability & Society*, 17, 4, 383–402.

Heinze, R. G. and Strünck, C. (2000) 'Die Verzinsung des socialen Kapitals. Freiwillinges Engagement im Strukturwandel', pp. 171–216 in U. Beck (ed.), *Die Zukunft von Arbeit und Demokratie*, Suhrkamp Verlag, Frankfurt-am-Main.

Hendry, C., Jones, A., Arthur, M. and Pettigrew, A. (1991) *Human Resource Development in Small to Medium Sized Enterprises*, Employment Department Research Paper 88, Sheffield.

Hendryx, M. S., Ahern, M. M., Lovrich, N. P. and McCurdy, A. H. (2002) 'Access to Health Care and Community Social Capital', *Health Services Research*, 37, 1, 87–103.

Henriksen, L. B. (1999) 'The Danish Furniture Industry – a case of tradition and change', pp. 233–58 in P. Karnøe, P. H. Kristensen and P. H. Andersen (eds), *Mobilising Influences and Generating Competencies: the remarkable success of small and medium-sized enterprises in the Danish business system*, Handelshøjskolens Forlag, Copenhagen.

Hibbitt, K., Jones, P., and Meegan, R. (2001) 'Tackling Social Exclusion: the role of social capital in urban regeneration on Merseyside – from mistrust to trust?' *European Planning Studies*, 9, 2, 141–61.

Hill, R.J. (1996) 'Learning to Transgress: a socio-historical conspectus of the American gay life world as a site of struggle and resistance', *Studies in the Education of Adults*, 28, 2, 253–79.

Hoffer, T., Greeley, A. and Coleman, J. S. (1985) 'Achievement and Growth in Public and Catholic Schools', *Sociology of Education*, 58, 2, 74–97.

Hyppä, M. and Mäki, J. (2001) 'Why do Swedish-speaking Finns have a longer active life? An area for social capital research', *Health Promotion International*, 16, 1, 55–64.

Inglehart, R (1997) *Modernisation and Postmodernisation: Cultural, Economic and Political Change in 43 Societies*, Princeton University Press, Princeton.

Ingram, P. and Roberts, P. W. (2000) 'Friendship among Competitors in the Sydney Hotel Industry', *American Journal of Sociology*, 106, 2, 387–423.

Jacobs, J. (1961) *The Death and Life of Great American Cities: the failure of town planning*, Random House, New York.

Jacques, M. (2002) 'The age of selfishness', *Guardian*, 5 October 2002, 24.

James, E. H. (2000) 'Race-Related Differences in Promotions and Support: underlying effects of human and social capital', *Organisation Science*, 11, 5, 493–508.

Jamieson, L. (1998) *Intimacy: personal relationships in modern societies*, Polity, Cambridge.

Jenkins, R. (1992) *Pierre Bourdieu*, London: Routledge.

Jones, T., McEvoy, D. and Barrett, G. (1993) 'Labour Intensive Practices in the Ethnic Minority Firm', in J. Atkinson, and D. Storey (eds), *Employment, the Small Firm and the Labour Market*, Routledge, London.

Karnøe, P. (1999) 'The Business Systems Framework and Danish SMEs', pp. 7–72 in P. Karnøe, P. H. Kristensen and P. H. Andersen (eds), *Mobilising Influences and Generating Competencies: the remarkable success of small and medium-sized enterprises in the Danish business system*, Handelshøjskolens Forlag, Copenhagen.

Kawachi, I., Kennedy, B. P. and Lochner, K. (1997a) 'Long Live Community: social capital as public health', *The American Prospect*, 35, 56–9.

Kawachi, I., Kennedy, B. P., Lochner, K., and Prothrow-Stith, D. (1997b) 'Social Capital, Income Inequality and Mortality', *American Journal of Public Health*, 87, 1491–98.

Kirchhöfer, D. (2000) *Informelles Lernen in alltäglichen Lebensführungen. Chance für berufliche Kompetenzentwicklung*, Qualifikations-Entwicklung-Management, Report 66, Berlin.

Klages, H. (2000) 'Engagement und Engagementpotential in Deutschland', pp. 151–70, in U. Beck (ed.), *Die Zukunft von Arbeit und Demokratie*, Suhrkamp Verlag, Frankfurt-am-Main.

Klein, N. (2000) *No Logo: taking aim at the brand bullies*, Flamingo, London.

Knack, S. and Keefer, P. (1997) 'Does Social Capital have an Economic Payoff? A cross-country investigation', *Quarterly Journal of Economics*, 112, 4, 1251–88.

Kniep, A. (2000) 'Wer nicht drin ist, ist draussen', *Spiegelreporter*, 8/2000, 18–27.

Kolankiewicz, G. (1996) 'Social Capital and Social Change', *British Journal of Sociology*, 47, 3, 427–41.

Korpi, T. (2001) 'Good Friends in Bad Times? Social networks and job search among the unemployed in Sweden', *Acta Sociologica*, 33, 2, 157–70.

Lall, S. (2000) 'Technological Change and Industrialisation in the Asian Newly Industrialising Economies: achievements and challenges', pp. 13–68 in L. Kim and R. R. Nelson (eds), *Technology, Learning and Innovation: experiences of newly industrialising economies*, Cambridge University Press, Cambridge.

Lauglo, J. (2000) 'Social Capital Trumping Class and Cultural Capital? Engagement with school among immigrant youth', pp. 142–67 in S. Baron, J. Field. and T. Schuller (eds), *Social Capital: critical perspectives*, Oxford University Press, Oxford.

Lazega, E. and Lebeaux, M.-O. (1995) 'Capital social et contrainte latérale', *Revue française de sociologie*, 36, 4, 759–77.

Le Bas, C., Picard, F., and Suchecki, B. (1998) 'Innovation technologique, comportement de reseaux et performances: une analyse sur données individuelles', *Revue d'Économie Politique*, 108, 5, 625–44.

Leadbeater, C. (1997) *The Rise of the Social Entrepreneur*, Demos, London.

Ledeneva, A. V. (1998) *Russia's Economy of Favours: Blat, networking and informal exchange*, Cambridge University Press, Cambridge.

Lemann, N. (1996) 'Kicking in Groups', *Atlantic Monthly*, April 1996, 22–6.

Leonard, M. (1998) 'The Long-Term Unemployed: informal economic activity and the underclass in Belfast – rejecting or reinstating the work ethic', *International Journal of Urban and Regional Research*, 22, 1, 42–59.

Lévesque, M. and White, D. (2001) 'Capital social, capital humain et sortie de l'aide sociale pour des prestataires de longue durée', *Canadian Journal of Sociology*, 26, 2, 167–92.

Lin, N. (2001) *Social Capital: a theory of social structure and action*, Cambridge University Press, Cambridge.

Lindenberg, S. (1996) 'Constitutionalism versus Relationalism: two versions of rational choice sociology', pp. 299–311 in J. Clark (ed.) *James S. Coleman*, Falmer, London.

Loizos, P. (2000) 'Are Refugees Social Capitalists?' pp. 124–41 in S. Baron, J. Field. and T. Schuller (eds), *Social Capital: critical perspectives*, Oxford University Press, Oxford.

Lovell A.M (2002) 'Risking Risk: the influence of types of capital and social networks on the injection practices of drug users', *Social Science and Medicine*, 55, 5, 803–21.

Lowndes, V. (2000) 'Women and Social Capital: a comment on Hall's 'Social Capital in Britain', *British Journal of Political Science*, 30, 4, 533–40.

Lowndes, V. and Wilson, D. (2001) 'Social Capital and Local Government: exploring the institutional design variable', *Political Studies*, 49, 4, 629–47.

Luhmann, N. (1988) 'Familiarity, Confidence, Trust: problems and alternatives', pp. 94–107 in D. Gambetta (ed.), *Trust: making and breaking co-operative relations*, Basil Blackwell, Oxford.

McClenaghan, P. (2000) 'Social Capital: exploring the theoretical foundations of community development education', *British Educational Research Journal*, 26, 5, 565–82.

McIlwaine, C. and Moser, C. O. N. (2001) 'Violence and Social Capital in Urban Poor Communities: perspectives from Colombia and Guatemala', *Journal of International Development*, 13, 965–84.

Macinko, J. and Starfield, B. (2001) 'The Utility of Social Capital in Research on Health Determinants', *Millbank Quarterly*, 79, 3, 387–427.

Maloney, W. (1999) 'Contracting Out the Participation Function: social capital and checkbook participation', pp. 108–19 in J. Van Deth, M. Maraffi,

K. Newton and P. Whiteley (eds), *Social Capital and European Democracy*, Routledge, London.

Maloney, W., Smith, G. and Stoker, G. (2000a) 'Social Capital and Associational Life', pp. 212–25 in S. Baron, J. Field. and T. Schuller (eds), *Social Capital: critical perspectives*, Oxford University Press, Oxford.

Maloney, W., Smith, G. and Stoker, G. (2000b) 'Social Capital and Urban Governance: adding a more contextualised "top-down" perspective', *Political Studies*, 48, 4, 802–20.

Maskell, P. (2000) 'Social Capital, Innovation and Competitiveness', pp. 111–23 in S. Baron, J. Field and T. Schuller (eds), *Social Capital: critical perspectives*, Oxford University Press, Oxford.

Maskell, P., Eskelinen, H., Hannibalsson, I., Malmberg, A. and Vatne, E. (1998) *Competitiveness, Localised Learning and Regional Development: specialisation and prosperity in small open economies*, Routledge, London.

Maskell, P. and Törnqvist, G. (1999) *Building a Cross-Border Learning Region: emergence of the North European Øresund region*, Handelshøjskolens Forlag, Copenhagen.

Matlay, H. (1997) *The Paradox of Training in the Small Business Sector*, PhD Thesis, University of Warwick, Coventry.

Melucci, A. (1996) *Challenging Codes: collective action in the information age*, Cambridge University Press, Cambridge.

Misztal, B. A. (1996) *Trust in Modern Societies*, Polity, Cambridge.

Misztal, B. A. (2000) *Informality: social theory and contemporary practice*, Routledge, London.

Mitchell, C. U. and LaGory, M. (2002) 'Social Capital and Mental Distress in an Impoverished Community', *City & Community*, 1, 2, 199–222.

Molyneux, M. (2002) 'Gender and the Silences of Social Capital: lessons from Latin America', *Development and Change*, 33, 2, 167–88.

Morrissey, M. and McGinn, P. (2001) *Evaluating Community Based and Voluntary Activity in Northern ireland: interim report*, Community Evaluation Northern Ireland, Belfast.

Morrow, V. (1999) 'Conceptualising Social Capital in Relation to the Well-being of Children and Young People: a critical review', *Sociological Review*, 744–65.

Mulholland, K. (1997) 'The Family, Enterprise and Business Strategies', *Work, Employment and Society*, 11, 4, 685–711.

Muntaner, C., Lynch, J. and Smith, G. D. (2000) 'Social Capital and the Third Way in Public Health', *Critical Public Health*, 10, 2, 107–24.

Muram, D., Hostetler, B., Jones, P., and Speck, C. (1995) 'Adolescent Victims of Sexual Assault', *Journal of Adolescent Health*, 17, 6, 372–5.

Murtagh, B. (2002) *Social Activity and Interaction in Northern Ireland: Northern Ireland Life and Times Survey Research Update 10*, Queen's University/University of Ulster, Belfast.

Narayan, D. and Pritchett, L. (1999) 'Social Capital: evidence and implications', pp. 269–95 in P. Dasgupta and I. Serageldin (eds), *Social Capital: a multifaceted perspective*, World Bank, Washington.

Neyer, F. J. (1995) 'Junge Erwachsene und ihre familiaren Netzwerke', *Zeitschrift für Sozialisationsforschung und Erziehungssoziologie*, 15, 3, 232–48.

OECD (Organisation for Economic Co-operation and Development) (2001a), *Investing in Competencies for All: Meeting of the OECD Education Ministers*, Paris, 3–4 April 2001, OECD, Paris.

OECD (Organisation for Economic Co-operation and Development) (2001b) *The Well-being of Nations: the role of human and social capital*, OECD, Paris.

Pahl, R. and Spencer, L. (1997) 'The Politics of Friendship', *Renewal*, 5, 3/4, 100–7.

Palloni, A., Massey, D.S., Ceballos, M., Espinosa, K. and Spittel, M. (2001) 'Social Capital and Intergenerational Migration: a test using information on family networks', *American Journal of Sociology*, 106, 5, 1262–98.

Parcel, T. and Menaghan, E. G. (1994) 'Early Parental Work, Family Social Capital and Early Childhood Outcomes', *American Journal of Sociology*, 99, 4, 972–1009.

Paxton, P. (1999) 'Is Social Capital Declining in the United States? A multiple indicator assessment', *American Journal of Sociology*, 105, 1, 88–127.

Performance and Innovation Unit (2002) *Social Capital: a discussion paper*, Cabinet Office, London.

Porter, M. E. (2000) 'Location, Competition and Economic Development: local clusters in a global economy', *Economic Development Quarterly*, 14, 1, 15–34.

Portes, A. (1998) 'Social Capital: its origins and applications in modern sociology', *Annual Review of Sociology*, 24, 1–24.

Portes, A. and Landolt, P. (2000) 'Social Capital: promise and pitfalls of its role in development', *Journal of Latin American Studies*, 32, 3, 529–47.

Prusack, L. and Cohen, D. (2001) 'How to Invest in Social Capital', *Harvard Business Review*, 79, 6, 87–93.

Putnam, R. D. (1993a) *Making Democracy Work: civic traditions in modern Italy*, Princeton University Press, Princeton.

Putnam, R. D. (1993b) 'The Prosperous Community: social capital and public life', *The American Prospect*, 4, 13, 11–18.

Putnam, R. D. (1995) 'Bowling Alone: America's declining social capital', *Journal of Democracy*, 6, 65–78.

Putnam, R. D. (1996) 'Who Killed Civic America?' *Prospect*, 7, 24, 66–72.

Putnam, R. D. (2000) *Bowling Alone: the collapse and revival of American community*, Simon and Schuster, New York.

Putnam, R. D. (2002) 'Bowling Together', *American Prospect*, 13, 3, accessed on 1 September 2002 at http://www.prospect.org/print/V13/3/putnam-r.html

Queen Elizabeth II (2002) 'Speech to both Houses of Parliament', 30 April 2002, Accessed on 1 September 2002 at http://www.goldenjubilee.info/News.jsp?NewsId=188

Raffo, C. and Reeves, M. (2000) 'Youth Transitions and Social Exclusion: developments in social capital theory', *Journal of Youth Studies*, 3, 2, 147–66.

Rankin, K. N. (2002) 'Social Capital, Microfinance, and the Politics of Development', *Feminist Economics*, 8, 1, 1–24.

Renzulli, L., Aldrich, H. and Moody, J. (2000) 'Family Matters: gender, networks and entrepreneurial outcomes', *Social Forces*, 79, 2, 523–46.

Ritzer, G. (1996) *Sociological Theory*, McGraw Hill, New York.

Robbins, D. (2000) *Bourdieu and Culture*, Sage, London.

Robison, L. J., Schmid, A.A. and Siles, M. E. (2002) 'Is Social Capital Really Capital?' *Review of Social Economy*, 60, 1, 1–21.

Rose, R. (1999) 'Getting Things Done in an Antimodern Society: social capital networks in Russia', pp 147–771 in P. Dasgupta and I. Serageldin (eds), *Social Capital: a multifaceted perspective*, World Bank, Washington.

Rosenfeld, R., Messner, S. F. and Baumer, E. (2001) 'Social Capital and Homicide', *Social Forces*, 80, 1, 283–309.

Rothstein, B. (2001) 'Social Capital in the Social Democratic Welfare State', *Politics and Society*, 29, 2, 207–41.

Russell, H. (1999) 'Friends in Low Places: gender, unemployment and sociability', *Work, Employment and Society*, 13, 2, 205–24.

Salmon, H. (2002) 'Social Capital and Neighbourhood Renewal', *Renewal*, 10, 2, 49–55.

Sampson, R. J. and Raudenbush, S. W. (1999) 'Systematic Social Observation of Public Spaces: a new look at disorder in urban neighbourhoods', *American Journal of Sociology*, 105, 3, 603–51.

Schuller, T. (2000) 'Human and Social Capital: the search for appropriate technomethodology', *Policy Studies*, 21, 1, 25–35.

Schuller, T., Baron, S. and Field, J. (2000) 'Social Capital: a review and critique', pp. 1–38 in Baron, S., Field, J. and Schuller, T. (eds), *Social Capital: critical perspectives*, Oxford University Press, Oxford.

Schulman, M. D. and Anderson, C. (1999) 'The Dark Side of the Force: a case study of restructuring and social capital', *Rural Sociology*, 64, 3, 351–72.

Schultz, T. W. (1961) 'Investment in Human Capital', *American Economic Review*, 51, 1–17.

Scott, J. (1991) *Social Network Analysis: a handbook*, Sage, London.

Senge, P. (1990) *The Fifth Discipline: the art and practice of the learning organisation*, Doubleday, New York.

Sennett, R. (1999) *The Corrosion of Character: The Personal Consequences of Work in the New Capitalism*, Norton, New York.

Serageldin, I. and Grootaert, C. (1999) 'Defining Social Capital: an integrating view', pp. 40–58 in P. Dasgupta and I. Serageldin (eds), *Social Capital: a multifaceted perspective*, World Bank, Washington.

Seyd, P. and Whiteley, P. (1992) *Labour's Grass Roots: the politics of party membership*, Clarendon Press, Oxford.

6, P. (1997) 'Social Exclusion: time to be optimistic', *Demos Collection*, 12, 3–9.

Skocpol, T. and Fiorina, M. (eds) (1999), *Civic Engagement in American Democracy*, Brookings Institution/Russell Sage Foundation, Washington/New York.

Smith, S. S. and Kulynch, J. (2002) 'It May be Social, but Why is it Capital? The social construction of social capital and the politics of language', *Politics & Society*, 30, 1, 149–86.

Stanton-Salazar, R. and Dornbusch, S. (1995) 'Social Capital and the Reproduction of Inequality: information networks among Mexican-origin high school students', *Sociology of Education*, 68, 2, 116–35.

Stephenson, S. (2001) 'Street Children in Moscow: using and creating social capital', *Sociological Review*, 49, 4, 530–47.

Streeck, W. (1999) *Verbände als soziales Kapital: Von Nutzen und Nutzung des Korporatismus in einer Gesellschaft im Wandel*, Max-Planck-Institut für Gesellschaftsforchung Working Paper 99/2, Cologne.

Summerskill, B. (2002) 'Selfish? Miserable? Not us, say UK teens', *Observer*, 21 July 2002, 3.

Swedberg, R. (1996) 'Analyzing the Economy: on the contribution of James S. Coleman', pp. 313–28 in J. Clark (ed.), *James S. Coleman*, Falmer Press, London.

Sztompka, P. (1999) *Trust: a sociological theory*, Cambridge University Press, Cambridge.

Thatcher, M. (1993) *The Downing Street Years*, HarperCollins, London.

Thompson, P. (2002) 'The Politics of Community', *Renewal*, 10, 2, 1–8.

Touraine, A. (1995) *Critique of Modernity*, Blackwell, Oxford.

Turkle, S. (1997) *Life on the Screen: identity in the age of the internet*, Touchstone, New York.

Unwin, L. (1996) 'Employer-led Realities: apprenticeship past and present', *Journal of Vocational Education and Training*, 48, 1, 57–68.

Urry, J. (2002) 'Mobility and Proximity', *Sociology*, 36, 2, 255–74.

Uslaner, E. M. (1999) 'Democracy and Social Capital', pp. 121–50 in M. E. Warren (ed.) *Democracy and Trust*, Cambridge University Press, Cambridge.

Van Deth, J. W. (2000) 'Interesting but Irrelevant: social capital and the saliency of politics in Western Europe', *European Journal of Political Research*, 37, 2, 115–47.

Viscarnt, J. J. (1998) 'EU Programmes: a "bridge" between education and employment', pp. 242–7 in A. Walther and B. Stauber (eds), *Lifelong Learning in Europe: options for the integration of living, learning and working*, Tübingen, Neuling Verlag.

Volker, B. and Flap, H. (1999) 'Getting Ahead in the GDR: social capital and status attainment under communism', *Acta Sociologica*, 42, 1, 17–34.

Walker, P., Lewis, J., Lingayah, S. and Sommer, F. (2000) *Prove It! Measuring the effect of neighbourhood renewal on local people*, Groundwork/ NewEconomics Foundation/Barclays PLC, London.

Wallis, J. and Dollery, B. (2002) 'Social Capital and Local Government Capacity', *Australian Journal of Public Administration*, 61, 3, 76–85.

Wann, M. (1995) *Building Social Capital: self-help in a twenty-first century welfare state*, Institute for Public Policy Research, London.

Warde, A. and Tampubolon, G. (2002) 'Social Capital, Networks and Leisure Consumption', *Sociological Review*, 50, 2, 155–80.

Warde, A., Martens, L. and Oben, W. (1999) 'Consumption and the Problem of Variety: cultural omnivorousness, social distinction and dining out', *Sociology*, 33, 1, 105–27.

Warren, M. E. (2001) 'Social Capital and Corruption', paper presented at EURESCO Conference on Social Capital, University of Exeter, 15–20 September 2001.

Wasserman, S. and Faust, K. (1994) *Social Network Analysis: methods and applications*, Cambridge University Press, Cambridge.

Wellman, B. (2001) 'Computer Networks as Social Networks', *Science*, 293, 2031–4.

Wellman, B. and Hampton, K. (1999) 'Living Networked in a Wired World', *Contemporary Sociology*, 28, 6, 648–54.

Wellman, B., Haase, A. Q., Witte, J., and Hampton, K. (2001) 'Does the Internet Increase, Decrease or Supplement Social Capital? Social networks, participation and community commitment', *American Behavioural Scientist*, 45, 3, 436–55.

Wennerås, C. and Wold, A. (1997) 'Nepotism and Sexism in Peer-review', *Nature*, 387, 341–3.

Whitehead, M. and Diderichsen, F. (2001) 'Social Capital and Health: tip-toeing through the minefield of evidence', *The Lancet*, 358, 9277, 165–6.

Whiteley, P. F. (2000) 'Economic Growth and Social Capital', *Political Studies*, 48, 3, 443–66.

Wilkinson, R. (1996) *Unhealthy Societies: the afflictions of inequality*, Routledge, London.

Wilson, P.A. (1997 'Building Social Capital: a learning agenda for the twenty-first century', *Urban Studies*, 34, 5/6, 745–60.

Woolcock, M. (1998) 'Social Capital and Economic Development: toward a theoretical synthesis and policy framework', *Theory and Society*, 27, 2, 151–208.

Woolcock, M. (2001) 'The Place of Social Capital in Understanding Social and Economic Outcomes', *Isuma: Canadian Journal of Policy Research*, 2, 1, 1–17.

World Bank (2001) *World Development Report 2000/2001 – Attacking Poverty*, World Bank/Oxford University Press, Washington/New York.

World Values Survey (2000) '2000–2001 World Values Survey Question-naire', http://wvs.isr.umich.edu/wvs-ques4.html (accessed 16 October 2001).

Young, M. (2002) 'Contrasting Approaches to the Role of Qualifications in the Promotion of Lifelong Learning, pp. 44–62 in K. Evans, P. Hodkinson and L. Unwin (eds), *Working to Learn: Transforming learning in the workplace*, Kogan Page, London.

Younge, G. (1999) 'The Death of Stephen Lawrence: the Macpherson Report', *Political Quarterly*, 70, 3, 329–34.

Zhao, Y. (2002) 'Measuring the Social Capital of Laid-off Chinese Workers', *Current Sociology*, 50, 4, 555–71.

INDEX